Life-study
of
Leviticus

Part One

Messages 18-35

Witness Lee

Living Stream Ministry
Anaheim, California

First Edition, 3,800 copies. March 1990.

ISBN 0-87083-504-1
(Messages 18-35, softcover)
ISBN 0-87083-488-6
(Complete set, softcover)

Published by

Living Stream Ministry
1853 W. Ball Road, Anaheim, CA 92804 U.S.A.
P. O. Box 2121, Anaheim, CA 92814 U.S.A.

Printed in the United States of America

CONTENTS

v

viii

Forerunner — The Surety of a Better Covenant — The High Priest Who Is Able to Save Us to the Uttermost — The Minister in the Heavens — The One Who Entered into the Holy of Holies in the Heavens and Obtained an Eternal Redemption — The One Appearing before God for Us — The Replacement of the Old Testament Offerings

LIFE-STUDY OF LEVITICUS

PART ONE—MESSAGE EIGHTEEN

THE SIN OFFERING
CHRIST FOR THE SIN OF GOD'S PEOPLE

(1)

Scripture Reading: Lev. 4:1-35; 1 John 1:5-9; Col. 1:12; Rom. 5:12; 7:17, 20; 8:3; John 1:14; 2 Cor. 5:21; John 3:14; Rom. 6:6; Heb. 2:14; 4:15; Gal. 5:19-21; John 12:31

In the foregoing messages we covered the first three of the five basic offerings—the burnt offering, the meal offering, and the peace offering. The fourth basic offering is the sin offering, and the fifth is the trespass offering. In this message we will begin to consider the sin offering.

THE SEQUENCE OF THE ARRANGEMENT
OF THE OFFERINGS

I admire the sequence of the arrangement of the five basic offerings. This sequence is not according to human thought, which would put the sin offering first. We know that we are sinful, and, as the first thing, we want our sin to be dealt with. After this, we might take the burnt offering, the meal offering, and the peace offering. The divine sequence is different from this. The divine sequence opens with the burnt offering, showing us that the primary thing with us should be that we are absolute for God. The burnt offering is followed by the meal offering, which shows us that we should take Christ as our life supply and live by Him daily. As the issue of taking Christ as the burnt offering and the meal offering, we have peace. Although we have peace, we still have certain problems—sin within and sins without—and these surely need to be dealt with.

The sequence of the offerings in Leviticus corresponds

to the sequence in chapter one of 1 John. Verse 5 says, "God is light, and in Him is no darkness at all." Verse 6 tells us that if we say that we have fellowship with the very God who is light and yet "walk in the darkness, we lie and are not practicing the truth." Verse 7 continues, "But if we walk in the light as He is in the light, we have fellowship with one another, and the blood of Jesus His Son cleanses us from all sin." This indicates that as we are having fellowship with God and enjoying Him, we will realize that between us and God there is a problem, and this problem is sin.

Sin and Sins

The New Testament deals with the problem of sin by using both the word *sin* in singular and the word *sins* in plural. Sin refers to the indwelling sin, which came through Adam into mankind from Satan (Rom. 5:12). It is dealt with in the second section of Romans, 5:12 to 8:13 (with the exception of 7:5, where *sins* is mentioned). Sins refer to the sinful deeds, the fruits of the indwelling sin, which are dealt with in the first section of Romans, 1:18 to 5:11. However, the singular sin in 1 John 1:7 with the adjective *all* does not denote the indwelling sin but every single sin we have committed (v. 10) after we have been regenerated. This sin defiles our purged conscience and needs to be cleansed away by the blood of the Lord Jesus in our fellowship with God.

Our sin, the indwelling sin in our nature (Rom. 7:17), has been taken care of by Christ as our sin offering (Lev. 4; Isa. 53:10; Rom. 8:3; 2 Cor. 5:21; Heb. 9:26). Our sins, our trespasses, have been taken care of by Christ as our trespass offering (Lev. 5; Isa. 53:11; 1 Cor. 15:3; 1 Pet. 2:24; Heb. 9:28). After our regeneration we still need to take Christ as our sin offering as indicated in 1 John 1:8 and as our trespass offering as indicated in verse 9.

First John 1:8 says, "If we say that we do not have sin, we are deceiving ourselves, and the truth is not in us." This verse speaks of indwelling sin, the sin which we inherited by our birth. This is the sin mentioned in Romans 5:12. If we say that, after we have been saved and regenerated, we do not have sin, we are self-deceived. Although we have been saved and regenerated and although we seek the Lord, love Him, and have fellowship with Him, we still have sin indwelling us. This is a fact. If we deny it, the truth is not in us.

First John 1:9 goes on to say, "If we confess our sins, He is faithful and righteous that He may forgive us our sins and cleanse us from all unrighteousness." This refers to the confession of our sins after our regeneration, not the confession of our sins before it. Here "sins" denotes our sinful deeds.

A Picture of the Sequence in 1 John

The sequence of the five offerings in Leviticus 1 through 5 is a picture of the sequence in 1 John 1. The burnt offering, the meal offering, and the peace offering bring us into fellowship with God. When we take Christ as our burnt offering before God and when we take Him as our daily life supply, we are brought into divine peace, and in this peace we enjoy the Triune God in fellowship. Therefore, the issue of our experience of the first three offerings is fellowship with God, who is light. In the light we see our failures, our mistakes, and our wrong attitude toward others. Eventually we realize not only that we have outward sins but also that sin dwells in our flesh. We even realize that we ourselves are sin. We have the deep realization that we are nothing but sin.

We may try to be good and do what is right. However, our situation turns out to be the opposite, and we learn to say with Paul, "Now it is no longer I that do it, but sin that dwells in me" (Rom. 7:17). Through our fellowship with God, who is light, we discover that we are sinful, that we have sin inwardly and sins outwardly. Inwardly we have a sinful "mother," and outwardly we have sinful deeds, which are the "children" of this sinful mother.

Galatians 5:19-21 speaks of the works of the flesh. These works include strife, jealousy, divisions, and parties.

Can we say that we are without strife and jealousy in our church life? We cannot say this. In the church life there may also be parties; that is, the saints may take sides with certain ones. This was the situation in Corinth. "Each of you says, I am of Paul, and I of Apollos, and I of Cephas, and I of Christ" (1 Cor. 1:12). If we have strife, jealousy, divisions, and parties in our church life or family life, we are living and acting in the flesh. If we say that we have fellowship with God and still have these works of the flesh, we are walking in darkness and we are self-deceived. If we have strife, jealousy, divisions, and parties in our church life, this means that our church life is in darkness. Likewise, if we say that we are in fellowship with God but are wrong in our attitude toward our husband or wife, we are self-deceived.

If we truly take Christ as our burnt offering to satisfy God and as our meal offering to be our daily food, we should be in the light and walk in the light. Then in the divine light we will see our failures and shortcomings. If we have an improper attitude toward our husband or wife, we will realize this and confess that it is wrong. If we have criticized certain brothers or taken sides with certain saints, we will realize that this also is wrong. Oh, may we all be willing to be enlightened and look to the Lord for light! If we say that we are enjoying the Lord, we must be in the light.

Colossians 1:12 tells us that Christ is the portion of the saints in the light. Christ is not the portion of the saints in darkness or in criticism or in parties. Where are we—in light or in darkness? We cannot enjoy Christ as the portion of the saints unless we are in the light.

After we enjoy Christ as the first three offerings, we need Him as the sin offering. As we are enjoying Him, we may say from the depths of our being, "Lord, I thank You that I am in Your presence. I love You, Lord, and I take You as my daily supply." Spontaneously the light will shine. The light may shine on a word we spoke to our spouse or on our criticizing of a certain brother. Immediately we will confess and ask the Lord to forgive us.

Quite often, as I was enjoying Him, the Lord enlightened me concerning my speaking well of a certain person and showed me that my speaking was from my flesh, from my natural being, not from my spirit. Therefore, I had to make confession to the Lord concerning my speaking well of others and of their good points.

Anything that is not in the spirit, whether it is good or evil, is of one source—the flesh. Criticizing others is of the flesh, and speaking well of others from our natural being is also of the flesh. Only what we do by walking, speaking, and behaving absolutely according to the spirit, setting our mind on the spirit (Rom. 8:6), is not of the flesh.

In Romans 8:4 Paul says that the righteous requirement of the law is fulfilled in those who walk according to the spirit. Paul does not say that when we do good things the righteous requirement of the law is fulfilled in us, for doing good things is not according to the tree of life but according to the tree of the knowledge of good and evil. Instead of trying to do good, we should simply walk according to the spirit. If we do not have the anointing in our spirit, we should not say anything good or bad. This is to walk in the spirit and to be delivered from the flesh.

THE FLESH AND THE CROSS

From the time I brought the Lord's recovery to the United States, I have stressed four matters: Christ, the Spirit, life, and the church. The burden concerning these matters has been very heavy. In this message, however, I am burdened to speak about the flesh and the cross. We need to know what the flesh is and how it is dealt with by the cross of Christ. In the Lord's recovery today, we need a word concerning the flesh and the cross. Our enjoyment of Christ may be full of leaven and honey and may also be lacking in salt. Therefore, I am burdened to minister salt, the cross, to the churches.

In speaking about the flesh and the cross, my concern is not doctrinal but experiential. As long as we live in this body, we still have the flesh. We need to be on the alert.

Yes, we have been buried with Christ in baptism, but Satan tries to resurrect what has been buried. Therefore, we need to be watchful, especially when we rise up in the morning. Having enjoyed the Lord in fellowship the night before, we may have slept peacefully. But when we rise up in the morning, the evil flesh may try to follow us. Although the flesh has been buried, it will still try to incite us to think negatively about our wife or husband or about certain brothers. We need to realize that such thoughts are a devilish resurrection of our flesh.

At such a time we need to pray, saying, "Lord, have mercy on me. I do not want to walk by this ugly flesh instigated by Your enemy. I want to enjoy You, Lord." Then, perhaps with tears, we may go on to pray, "Father, I take Your Son, my dear Lord, as my burnt offering. I cannot be absolutely for You, but I can enjoy such a life in Him. I take Him as my burnt offering to offer to You, Father. I also take Him as my daily food." This will bring us into the enjoyment of Christ as the peace offering. Then, as we are before the Lord, we will be enlightened and exposed, and we will see what kind of person we are. At this point we need the dear Lord Jesus as our sin offering. This is to take as our sin offering the very Christ who is our burnt offering, meal offering, and peace offering. This sequence is not a doctrinal matter. Rather, it is according to our personal, and often painful, experience.

Whenever we have the experience of enjoying peace with the Triune God, we will realize our need of the sin offering. We will confess to the Lord, saying, "Father, I have never realized that I am so sinful. I am not only sinful—I am sin. Sin dwells in my flesh, and I am a totality of sin. I surely need my Lord Jesus to be my sin offering. How I treasure Him as my sin offering!"

Whatever issues from the flesh is sin. Whether we criticize others or praise them, both have their source in the flesh and are sin. The only way to deal with this flesh is the cross, the salt. We need much salt in our daily life, family life, and church life. Only when we have the salt will the "germs" become inactive. The church life today needs "pest control," the killing of germs by the experience of the cross. This killing is the Lord's mercy; it is the Lord's merciful salvation to us.

SIN, THE FLESH, SATAN, AND THE WORLD

According to the New Testament, there are four things that cannot be separated: sin, the flesh, Satan, and the world. These four things are one.

Three Denotations of Flesh in the Bible

In the Bible the word *flesh* has different denotations. First, the flesh denotes the meat of the human body (Gen. 2:21). Second, in Genesis 6:3 the flesh denotes fallen mankind. This is also the denotation in Romans 3:20, where Paul says that "by the works of law no flesh shall be justified" before God. Third, the flesh denotes the corrupted body (Rom. 7:18). God created the human body. But after the body was corrupted, it became the flesh. In contrast to a spiritual person, who lives in the spirit, and a natural person, who lives in the soul, a fleshly, or fleshy, person lives in the lusts of the flesh (1 Cor. 3:1, 3; 2:14).

The Word Becoming Flesh

John 1:14 says, "The Word became flesh." What is the meaning of *flesh* here? According to the context of the whole Gospel of John, the flesh in 1:14 denotes fallen, sinful man. God, the Word, became a fallen, sinful man *but only in likeness.* Paul makes this clear when he tells us in Romans 8:3 that God sent "His own Son in the likeness of the flesh of sin." This proves that the flesh in John 1:14 is the flesh of sin. The meaning of the incarnation is that God became a sinful man *in likeness.* In his note on this verse, Dr. Ryrie says, "Jesus Christ was unique, for He was God from all eternity and yet joined Himself to sinful humanity in the incarnation."

The type of the brass serpent (John 3:14; Num. 21:4-9) indicates that Christ did not have the flesh of sin but only the likeness of the flesh of sin. When the children of Israel sinned against God, they were bitten by serpents and were dying. Actually, in the sight of God, they were dead. God told Moses to lift up a brass serpent on their behalf for God's judgment, that by looking upon that brass serpent they might be saved and live. The brass serpent was their savior. This is a type. In John 3:14 the Lord Jesus applied this type to Himself, showing that when He was in the flesh, He was, to use Paul's words, in the likeness of the flesh of sin, which likeness was the form of the brass serpent. It had the form of the serpent but not the poison. Christ was made in the likeness of the flesh of sin, but He had no participation in the sin of the flesh (2 Cor. 5:21; Heb. 4:15). The brass serpent is a type of Christ as our Savior. "As Moses lifted up the serpent in the wilderness, even so must the Son of Man be lifted up; that everyone who believes in Him may have eternal life" (John 3:14-15).

The Lamb of God,
the Brass Serpent, and the Grain of Wheat

In the Gospel of John three figures are used to describe Christ in His death: the Lamb of God (1:29), the brass serpent (3:14), and a grain of wheat (12:24). These figures describe three aspects of Christ as our Savior. In dealing with sin, He is the Lamb. In dealing with Satan, the old serpent, He is the brass serpent, the One in the likeness of the flesh of sin. In releasing the divine life to produce us as the many sons of God, He is the grain of wheat. Therefore, He is the Lamb-Savior, He is the Serpent-Savior, and He is the Grain-Savior. We have Him as our Savior in three aspects—to deal with our sin, to destroy the old serpent, and to produce us as the many sons of God.

I believe that Adam, the man created by God, was handsome. The Lord Jesus, on the contrary, had no comeliness or beauty and was not outwardly attractive (Isa. 53:2). He was a man exhausted from all kinds of sorrow (Isa. 53:3). Our Lord became a fallen man in likeness. However, when the Lord Jesus was on the cross, God counted that likeness as real.

Sin in the Flesh, the Old Man,
Satan, and the World Dealt With
through the Death of Christ on the Cross

The New Testament emphasizes the fact that Christ was crucified in the flesh and died in the flesh. He did not die in anything other than the God-condemned flesh. Romans 8:3 says, "God sending His own Son in the likeness of the flesh of sin and concerning sin, condemned sin in the flesh." When the Lord Jesus was crucified in the flesh, God condemned sin in the flesh. Sin is not merely a matter; sin is a person, and this person needed to be condemned. Through the Lord's death on the cross, God condemned sin in the flesh. This means that when the flesh was crucified, sin in the flesh was condemned.

Romans 6:6 tells us that our old man was crucified with Christ. Our old man is in the flesh. Because Christ was crucified in the flesh, our old man, who is in the flesh, could be crucified with Him. Our old man was crucified with Christ in the flesh.

Through the death of Christ not only was sin condemned and not only was our old man crucified, but also Satan, the Devil, was destroyed (Heb. 2:14). Furthermore, through the cross of Christ the world was judged and the ruler, the prince, of the world was cast out (John 12:31). Therefore, through the death of Christ on the cross four things were dealt with: sin in the flesh, the old man, Satan, and the world. This means that through Christ's death in His flesh all negative things were dealt with.

We need to have this realization whenever we take Christ as our sin offering. The sin offering means that sin in the flesh has been condemned, that our old man has been crucified, that Satan has been destroyed, and that the world has been condemned and the ruler of the world cast out.

We all need to learn to take Christ as such a sin offering. When we enter into fellowship with the Triune God through Christ as the burnt offering, the meal offering, and the peace offering, then we need to apply Christ as our sin offering.

LIFE-STUDY OF LEVITICUS

PART ONE — MESSAGE NINETEEN

THE SIN OFFERING
CHRIST FOR THE SIN OF GOD'S PEOPLE

(2)

Scripture Reading: Lev. 4:1-7, 13-18, 22-25, 27-30, 32-34

In this message we will cover a number of matters related to the sin offering.

I. THE SIGNIFICANCE OF THE SIN OFFERING

A. For the Sin of Ignorance

A number of times Leviticus 4 speaks of the sin of ignorance (vv. 1-2, 13, 22, 27). A sin of ignorance refers to a mistake, error, or oversight; that is, it denotes sinning unintentionally. Although we may not have the intention to sin, we nevertheless sin unintentionally.

The sin of ignorance in Leviticus 4 signifies the sin in our fallen nature, the indwelling sin. The sin which we inherited from Adam dwells in our flesh. Many times we sin unintentionally. These sins come from the indwelling sin. Sin came in through Adam's fall and entered into the human race (Rom. 5:12). Therefore, with all human beings there is something called sin.

In Romans 7 sin is personified, because it can dwell in us (v. 17), kill us (v. 11), and do many things in us. Thus, sin is a living person. We cannot find a verse which says that sin is Satan himself. However, the Bible indicates that sin is the nature of Satan. Since sin is the nature of Satan, sin is actually Satan himself.

Sin entered the human race at the time of Adam's fall. This means that Adam's fall opened the gate for sin, which is the nature of Satan and even Satan himself, to come into our being. Romans 7 tells us clearly that sin dwells in our flesh (vv. 17, 20, 23). We have often wanted to do good, for example to honor our parents or regard our brother, yet the outcome was just the opposite. We sinned unintentionally, doing something that we had no intention of doing. Because Paul had this kind of experience, he could say, "It is no longer I that do it but sin that dwells in me" (Rom. 7:20b).

In Romans 7 we can see two persons. One person does not want to sin, and the other person, who is within the first person, sins. This indicates that Paul was living a life of two persons—a life of himself, Saul of Tarsus, and a life of something that is called sin. These two persons lived together, but not willingly. Sometimes they were good friends, and sometimes they fought with each other.

Romans 7 is a picture of our experience not only before we were saved but even today. Have you not discovered that there is a war going on within you? On the one hand, we may say, "I love the church." On the other hand, something within us says, "I do not like the church." Sometimes we may say, "I love all the saints. All of them are dear and loveable." However, there may be a certain elder whom we cannot love. There is a fighting within us. We aspire to be holy, but the outcome is not holiness. All day long we commit sins of ignorance.

We may have been Christians for years, but there is still a war going on within us. We may want to be perfect, but we do many things that are sins of ignorance. Therefore, since sin dwells within us and we commit sins of ignorance, we are not trustworthy.

Anything that is done out of our flesh is sin. In the eyes of God, even our love that is out of the flesh is sin. Not only the bad things are sin, but even the good things that are out of the flesh are sin. It is the source, not the outcome or issue, that counts. This is the reason Galatians 5:24 says, "They who are of Christ Jesus have crucified the flesh with the passions and the lusts."

According to the human view, the flesh may seem to be good as well as bad. But whether we are good, bad, or in the middle, as long as we are flesh we are sin. The flesh is altogether one with sin (Rom. 8:3), and sin is altogether one with Satan. Actually, sin is Satan. Furthermore, Satan is one with the world, and the world is one with the prince of the world (John 12:31). These five things are one matter: the flesh, sin, Satan, the world, and the prince (the authority or power) of the world.

Today's world is related to the flesh, sin, Satan, and the prince of the world. The word *prince* here implies authority or power. The world is actually the struggle for power. Every person and every nation are struggling for power. Everywhere there is competition, rivalry, for power. In the universities both the professors and the students are struggling for power. For example, a professor may say that he is trying to help society or that he wants to invent something to benefit society. Actually he, along with everyone else, is struggling for power. This struggle for power is the result, the issue, of the flesh, sin, Satan, the world, and the prince of the world.

Galatians 5:16-26 speaks of the struggle between the flesh and the Spirit. Verse 26, the concluding verse of this section, says, "Let us not become vainglorious, provoking one another, envying one another." In this verse is the struggle for vainglory. This indicates that even in the church life there may be the struggle for vainglory. This is proved by the fact that Paul's word here was written to churches, to the churches of Galatia (Gal. 1:2), which was a province of the ancient Roman Empire. We all seek vainglory. If this were not our situation, Paul would not have needed to say this word to us. We may think that the things mentioned in 5:16-26 existed among the churches of Galatia but are not among us today. However, we should not read these verses as applying to them alone; we should include ourselves when we read such verses. Just as we apply John 3:16 to ourselves, so we should also apply Galatians 5:16-26.

The sin offering has a broad denotation. It deals not only with sin itself but also with our flesh, with Satan, the evil one in our flesh, with the world, and with the struggle for power. According to the Bible, sin is involved with these four things.

Satan is the prince of the world. Satan may even be proud of being such a prince. Isaiah 14 reveals that although he was close to God, he was not satisfied. He wanted to be above God or at least to be in rivalry with Him. Therefore, when the Bible condemns sin, it condemns Satan and also the flesh, the world, and the struggle for power. Everything that is happening on earth is related to the struggle for power. All the good speeches, lectures, and explanations given by men are just cloaks to cover the struggle for power.

B. God Sending His Son in the Likeness of the Flesh of Sin and concerning Sin, Condemning Sin in the Flesh on the Cross of Christ

The sin offering also signifies that God, sending His own Son in the likeness of the flesh of sin and concerning sin, condemned sin in the flesh on the cross of Christ (Rom. 8:3). Christ became flesh; that is, He came in the likeness of the flesh of sin (John 1:14). Furthermore, God made Christ, who did not know sin, sin on our behalf on the cross (2 Cor. 5:21). While Christ was on the cross, He was judged in the form of the serpent for our sin (John 3:14). In this way God condemned sin in the flesh on the cross of Christ.

II. THE EFFICACY OF THE SIN OFFERING

The efficacy of the sin offering is not just in the fact that it deals with sin. The result is far greater. In the sin offering, the fallen man, the old man, included in the flesh of Christ, is dealt with (Rom. 6:6); sin in the nature of fallen man is condemned (Rom. 8:3); Satan, sin itself, is destroyed (Heb. 2:14); the world is judged; and the prince of the world is cast out (John 12:31). This is the revelation in the holy Word concerning the efficacy of the sin offering.

If we see this revelation, we will see that taking Christ as our sin offering is not simply a matter of confessing our sin and having it dealt with. Taking Christ as our sin offering also means that our old man, Satan, the world, and the struggle for power are dealt with. Since all these things are included in the sin offering, taking Christ as our sin offering is not a simple matter but a matter that involves the fallen man, sin in the nature of fallen man, Satan, the world, and the struggle for power.

III. DIFFERENT KINDS OF CATTLE FOR THE SIN OFFERING

In Leviticus 4 there are different kinds of cattle for the sin offering.

A. A Young Bull, a Buck of the Goats, a Ewe of the Goats, or a Female Lamb

The sin offering may be a young bull, a buck of the goats, a ewe of the goats, or a female lamb (Lev. 4:3, 14, 23, 28, 32). This signifies that Christ as the sin offering is experienced by different people in different degrees. In Himself as the sin offering, Christ does not differ in size. He is always the same. However, our realization, presentation, and application of Christ as the sin offering may differ in degree.

The size of Christ as our sin offering depends on the degree to which we take Christ as our sin offering. We may take Christ as our sin offering to a lower degree or to a higher degree. One brother may take Christ as his sin offering to deal only with his sin, not realizing that sin implies the flesh. A second brother may realize that the sin offering implies the flesh but may not realize that it also implies dealing with Satan. If we see that as long as sin dwells in us, the flesh, Satan, the world, and the struggle for power are also present, we can offer Christ as a large bull.

B. Without Blemish

Leviticus 4 tells us that the sin offering is without blemish (vv. 3, 23, 28, 32). This signifies that Christ is without sin (2 Cor. 5:21; Heb. 4:15).

IV. LAYING HANDS ON THE HEAD OF THE OFFERING

Leviticus 4 speaks of laying hands on the head of the offering (vv. 4, 15, 24, 29, 33). This signifies the union of the offerer with the offering.

V. THE OFFERING SLAUGHTERED BEFORE JEHOVAH

The sin offering was slaughtered before Jehovah (vv. 4, 15, 24). This signifies that Christ as the sin offering was slaughtered before God, that He was recognized by God (Isa. 53:10a).

VI. THE BLOOD OF THE SIN OFFERING

The blood of the sin offering has four different kinds of effects.

A. Some of the Blood Brought into the Tent of Meeting and Sprinkled Seven Times toward the Veil of the Holy of Holies

Some of the blood of the sin offering was brought into the tent of meeting and sprinkled seven times toward the veil of the Holy of Holies (Lev. 4:5-6, 16-17). This signifies that the blood of Christ has been brought into the Holy of Holies in the heavens for our redemption (Heb. 9:12). Christ's blood covers our situation with God in the Holy of Holies.

B. Some of the Blood Put upon the Horns of the Incense Altar

Some of the blood was put upon the horns of the incense altar (Lev. 4:7a, 18a). This signifies that the redemption of Christ's blood is effective for us to contact God in prayer (Heb. 10:19). This is why we need to pray through the blood, contacting God in our prayer through the blood.

C. Some of the Blood Put upon the Horns of the Altar of Burnt Offering

Some of the blood was put upon the horns of the altar of burnt offering (Lev. 4:25a, 30, 34a). This signifies that the blood of Christ is effective for our redemption. The blood of Christ as the sin offering brings us into the presence of God, that is, into the Holy of Holies; it gives us the position and right to contact God in prayer; and it is effective for our redemption.

D. All the Rest of the Blood Poured Out at the Base of the Altar of Burnt Offering

All the rest of the blood was poured out at the base of the altar of burnt offering (4:7b, 18b, 25b, 30b, 34b). This signifies the blood of Christ at the standing of the cross for the peace in our conscience that we are redeemed and accepted by God.

LIFE-STUDY OF LEVITICUS

PART ONE—MESSAGE TWENTY

THE SIN OFFERING
CHRIST FOR THE SIN OF GOD'S PEOPLE

(3)

Scripture Reading: Lev. 4:8-15, 19, 21, 26, 31, 35; 6:25; 16:3, 5

Before we consider more aspects of the sin offering, I would like to give a further word concerning sin. In the New Testament sin is a personified matter. It is not something small but is a very crucial matter.

In this universe there are two sources. One is God, and the other is Satan, God's enemy and adversary (the word *Satan* means adversary). Satan became God's enemy and adversary when he entered into a struggle with God for power (Isa. 14). Satan also tempted the Lord Jesus with respect to power (Luke 4:5-7). The whole universe today is a matter of the power struggle between Satan and God. All the world follows Satan and has become a part of this evil struggle. Therefore, under the influence of Satan, all of humankind is engaged in a power struggle. For example, the employees in a certain corporation may be striving for a promotion. This is a small part of the universal power struggle, a struggle that can be found everywhere.

This power struggle is one of the five items whose aggregate is sin. These items are the flesh, sin, Satan, the world, and the prince of the world. The prince of the world signifies the struggle for power. Every human being, including little children, likes to be a prince, a leader, and everywhere on earth today there is a power struggle. As we will see, this power struggle is related to the sin offering.

When we repented to the Lord and received Him as our Savior, we were enlightened to see that we are evil and under God's condemnation. The more we love the Lord, the

more we realize that we are evil. The more a believer prays,
the more he feels that he is too evil. Eventually, we are
brought to the realization that even today as a Christian
seeking after the Lord we are nothing but a totality of sin.
We are not only evil and sinful—we are the totality of sin.

If we realize that we are sinful and begin to confess our
sins, we may find that the more we confess, the more there
is to confess. This was my experience in 1935. One day,
having the deep sense that I needed to be alone with the
Lord, I went to a secluded place, kneeled down, prayed, and
began to confess my sins. My confession went on for a long
time. Prior to that time, I did not know how sinful I was or
how many sins I had. I saw that everything I had done
since my youth was sinful, and I made a thorough
confession to the Lord.

We need to pray and take the Lord Jesus as our burnt
offering, as the One who is absolute for God. Enjoying
Christ as the burnt offering will lead us to take Him as our
life supply, as our meal offering, which is Christ in His
humanity becoming our daily food. We need to enjoy Him
until we feel that we have peace with God, with ourselves,
and with everyone. Immediately we will be in the light,
and the light will shine within us, upon us, and around us.
Then we will realize that we have sinned and that we are
sin. This is the experience in 1 John chapter one. God is
light (v. 5). In order to have fellowship with Him, we must
walk in the light as He is in the light. If we do this, we will
realize that we have something called sin (vv. 7-8).

The sin spoken of in 1 John 1 is not an insignificant
matter. Sin is God's enemy, Satan himself, and it involves
the power struggle between Satan and God. This power
struggle includes us; we are involved in it.

Why are we not absolute for God? We are not absolute
for God because something within us is for ourselves and
not for God. This is the struggle. A sister may experience
this struggle while shopping in a department store. She
may want to buy a particular item, but she senses that the
Lord does not agree. She begs the Lord to give her
permission to make the purchase this one time. Her

begging is actually a sign of a struggle between her and the Lord. Satan is hidden within such a struggle.

We struggle with the Lord about many things. We love the Lord, we attend the church meetings, and we participate fully in the church life. On the surface everything appears to be fine. However, only we ourselves know how much we are in a struggle with God day after day. God wants us to be absolute for Him, but we may be willing to be absolute for Him only to a certain degree. We may criticize others for not being absolute for God, but how much are we absolute for Him? Instead of being utterly absolute for God, we engage in a power struggle with Him.

Who can say that he is absolute for God? Since none of us is absolute for God, we need Christ as our burnt offering. Only Christ is absolute for God.

In dealing with sin, Paul was eventually brought to something deeper—not merely to sin itself but to the law of sin (Rom. 7:25; 8:2). Many Christians do not realize that there is such a thing as the law of sin. Do you know what the law of sin is? The law of sin is simply the spontaneous power, strength, and energy to struggle with God. Something within us is living and active; it is crouching in our inner being, watching over us. Whenever we have even a little thought of being for God, something within us rises up to take us over. This is the law of sin. In his experience, Paul found out not only that sin dwelt in his flesh, but also that within him there was a natural power, strength, and energy to resist whenever he desired to be for God. This made him a wretched man (Rom. 7:24). This is the law of sin as the deeper meaning of sin.

We have often been defeated by this thing that is crouching within us. For example, we may want to love the Lord, but spontaneously the law of sin operates within us, and after a short time the thought of loving the Lord disappears.

It was through his experience with the commandment regarding greed, or coveting, that Paul discovered the law of sin (Rom. 7:7-8). All of the Ten Commandments deal with outward matters except the commandment not to covet. This commandment touches the greed within us. Paul did not want to be greedy, but he could not help it. When he tried to obey this commandment, something within him rose up and wrought in him "coveting of every kind." Paul was thus a victim of the law of sin.

We should not take Christ as our sin offering in a superficial way. Rather, we should take Him as our sin offering to a deeper extent. This will remake our entire being.

Now that we have seen that sin involves a power struggle and that the law of sin is the spontaneous power, strength, and energy to struggle with God, let us go on to consider some further aspects of the sin offering in Leviticus 4.

VII. ALL THE FAT
THAT COVERS THE INWARDS
AND THAT IS ON THE INWARDS,
THE TWO KIDNEYS AND THE FAT ON THEM,
AND THE APPENDAGE ON THE LIVER
BEING BURNED ON THE ALTAR OF BURNT OFFERING

All the fat that covers the inwards and that is on the inwards, the two kidneys and the fat on them, and the appendage on the liver were burned on the altar of burnt offering (Lev. 4:8-10, 19, 26, 31, 35). This signifies that the inwards of Christ as the tender and sweet part are offered to God for His satisfaction that He may be willing to forgive us.

These parts of the sin offering were burned on the altar of burnt offering. This indicates that God's acceptance of the sin offering is based on the burnt offering. Without the burnt offering as the base, the sin offering cannot be accepted by God.

VIII. THE WHOLE OFFERING,
INCLUDING ITS HIDE, ALL ITS FLESH,
WITH ITS HEAD, LEGS, INWARDS, AND DUNG,
TO BE BURNED OUTSIDE THE CAMP

The whole offering, including its hide, all its flesh, with its head, legs, inwards, and dung, was burned outside the camp (vv. 11-12, 21). This signifies that Christ as the sin offering suffered reproach outside the Jewish religion—a human organization (Heb. 13:11-13). Christ was crucified outside Jerusalem, which was considered a camp representing the Jewish religious organization.

A. At a Clean Place

The sin offering was burned at a clean place. This signifies the place where Christ as the sin offering was rejected by man and where man's sin is cleared.

B. At the Place
Where the Ashes Are Poured Out

The place where the sin offering was burned was a place where the ashes were poured out.

1. The Ashes of the Burnt Offering

The ashes of the burnt offering signify God's recognition and acceptance of the offerings. How do we know that God has accepted the burnt offering? We know this by the fact that it has been turned to ashes. Because the ashes are a sign that God has received the burnt offering, the ashes are dear.

2. For the Offerers' Assurance and Peace

The ashes are for the offerers' assurance and peace in their heart concerning God's redemption of their sin. The ashes are a sign assuring us that God has accepted our sin offering for the redemption of our sin.

IX. WHEN ALL THE CONGREGATION
OF ISRAEL SINNED IGNORANTLY,
THE ELDERS WERE TO REPRESENT THE ASSEMBLY
TO OFFER THE SIN OFFERING

When all the congregation of Israel sinned ignorantly, the elders were to represent the assembly to offer the sin offering (vv. 13-15). This signifies that the elders of the church may represent the church to offer Christ as its sin offering.

X. THE SIN OFFERING BEING SLAUGHTERED
IN THE PLACE WHERE
THE BURNT OFFERING IS SLAUGHTERED

The sin offering was to be slaughtered in the place where the burnt offering was slaughtered (Lev. 6:25). This indicates that the sin offering is based upon the burnt offering, and it signifies that Christ is the sin offering for us based upon His being the burnt offering. Christ must be the burnt offering for God's satisfaction that He might be qualified to be our sin offering.

If we have never enjoyed Christ as the burnt offering, we cannot realize how sinful we are. We heard the gospel and repented, realizing that we are sinful. But we cannot know how sinful we are until we enjoy Christ as our burnt offering. The burnt offering means that mankind, created by God for the purpose of expressing and representing Him, should be for nothing other than God and should be absolutely for God. However, we are not absolutely for God. We need to realize this and take Christ as our burnt offering. Only when we enjoy Christ as our burnt offering will we realize how sinful we are.

If we realize how sinful we are, we will know that our love as well as our hate may be sinful. Ethically, to hate others is wrong and to love others is right. We may think that in the eyes of God loving others is acceptable and hating others is not acceptable. But in the eyes of God we hate people for ourselves and also love people for ourselves, not for God. From this point of view, loving others is just as sinful as hating others. Whatever we do for ourselves and not for God—whether it is moral or immoral, good or evil, a matter of love or of hate—is sinful in the eyes of God. As long as you do a certain thing for yourself, it is sinful.

God created us that we might be for Him. He created us to be His expression and His representation. He did not create us for ourselves. But we live independently of Him. When we hate others, we are independent of God, and when we love others, we are also independent of God. This means that in God's sight our hatred and our love are the same.

Furthermore, neither our hatred nor our love is from our spirit. Rather, both our hatred and our love are from our flesh, and both are from the tree of the knowledge of good and evil. The tree of the knowledge of good and evil signifies Satan. We should not think that only doing evil is of Satan and doing good is not. Doing both good and evil may be of Satan. We need to realize that anything we do out of ourselves, whether good or evil, is for ourselves, and since it is for ourselves it is sin.

I would point out once again that sin involves a power struggle. We may love others for ourselves—for our name, position, benefit, and pride. This kind of love is in the power struggle with God. We need to pray, "Lord, save me from doing anything for my pride, for my name, for my promotion, for my benefit, for my interests." This is to be saved from the power struggle with God. When we love others for our name and promotion, we are not for God. This kind of love is of Satan; it is in the flesh, and it is sin. Whatever is in the flesh is sin, whatever is sin in our flesh is Satan, and whatever is done there by Satan is the power struggle.

Some may wonder about our love as Christian parents for our children. Our love for our children may be in the flesh. The New Testament charges us to raise up our children in the Lord. However, we may raise up our children for ourselves and our future. This is sin.

Even in the church life we may do things that are not for God but for ourselves. We may do something that is very good, yet deep within our hidden intention is to do that good thing for ourselves. This is sinful. For example, in giving a testimony or in praying, we may want everyone to say "amen" to us. We may offer a high, spiritual prayer, but our aim in doing so may be to receive the "amens." Such a prayer is sinful because it is not absolutely for God. From this we see that even in our prayer there is the power struggle with God. We desire position, not God.

Because we may have hidden motives in doing spiritual things, the Lord Jesus spoke concerning those who do things apparently for God but actually for the purpose of advancing themselves. Therefore, He said, "Take heed not to do your righteousness before men to be gazed at by them" (Matt. 6:1). Concerning giving alms He said, "Let not your left hand know what your right hand is doing" (v. 3). Concerning prayer He went on to say, "When you pray, you shall not be as the hypocrites; for they love to pray standing in the synagogues and on the street corners that they may appear to men" (v. 5). Concerning fasting He said, "Whenever you fast, do not be as the hypocrites of a sad countenance; for they disguise their faces so that they may appear to men to be fasting" (v. 16). Even in doing righteousness, giving alms, praying, and fasting there may be a power struggle with God. To do these things for ourselves and not for God is sinful in His eyes. Those who do such things for themselves give no ground to God; instead, all the ground is for themselves.

To take Christ as the sin offering is very deep. The experience of the sin offering is altogether related to our enjoyment of the Lord Jesus as our burnt offering. The more we love the Lord and enjoy Him, the more we will know how evil we are. Sometimes, when we love the Lord to the uttermost, we may feel that there is no place to hide ourselves. Paul had such a realization concerning himself. When he was seeking the Lord, he saw that there was nothing good in himself.

XI. FOR THE PRIESTS' SERVICE, THE SIN OFFERING BEING FOLLOWED BY THE BURNT OFFERING

For the priests' service, the sin offering is followed by the burnt offering (Lev. 16:3, 5). This signifies that we, as the priests of God, after enjoying Christ as the sin offering, must take Him as the burnt offering that we may live Him for God's satisfaction.

On the one hand, the sin offering is based on the burnt offering. On the other hand, the burnt offering follows the sin offering. The more we enjoy the Lord Jesus as our burnt offering, the more we realize that we are sinful. Then we take Him as our sin offering more deeply than ever, and this causes us to enjoy Him more as the burnt offering. Hence, the burnt offering is before our enjoyment of the sin offering and also after it.

The only way we can know ourselves thoroughly is to enjoy Christ as the burnt offering. By enjoying Christ as our burnt offering, we will realize that we are not for God absolutely. We may be for God to some degree, even to a large degree, but we still reserve something for ourselves.

Whenever we touch the holy things, the spiritual things, and the service of God in the church life, we must bring the sin offering with us. This is clearly revealed in the Old Testament type. Whenever God's people did something with God, even the most holy things, they needed the sin offering. We also need the sin offering today because we are not clean and pure and we are not absolutely for God. Who among us can say that he is absolutely for God? No one can say this. Therefore, in all that we do for the Lord, we need the sin offering. Even in speaking for the Lord, we need to take Christ as our sin offering, hiding ourselves in Him and asking Him to cover us with His precious blood.

First, the Lord saves us, and then He attracts us to love Him, to take Him, and to enjoy Him. By taking Him and enjoying Him as the burnt offering, our sinfulness is exposed, and we see that we are not absolutely for God as He is. Others in the church life may appreciate us, but inwardly we know that we are not good, that we are not absolute for God. We may love the church and seemingly we have given everything for the church, but we are not absolute for God. There are still reservations within us.

By enjoying the Lord as the burnt offering and the meal offering, we realize that we are sinful. So we take Him as the sin offering and then as the trespass offering. This is what we see in chapter one of 1 John. As we are enjoying the Triune God in the divine fellowship, we realize that we still have sin inwardly and that we have committed sins outwardly. We then receive the cleansing of the precious blood. This becomes a cycle. The more we are cleansed, the more we enter into fellowship with the Triune God; the more we enjoy this fellowship, the more we are enlightened;

and the more we are enlightened, the more we realize that we are sinful, even sin itself. It is by this cycle that we are delivered and saved from our self. Actually, we are delivered and saved from sin, from the flesh, from Satan, from the world, from the prince of the world, and from the power struggle. The more we enjoy Christ, the less power struggle we will have with God. Eventually we will give every inch to Him.

LIFE-STUDY OF LEVITICUS

PART ONE — MESSAGE TWENTY-ONE

THE TRESPASS OFFERING
CHRIST FOR THE SINS OF GOD'S PEOPLE

(1)

Scripture Reading: Lev. 5:1-10; 7:2

In this message we will begin to consider the trespass offering. We may think that, as the last of the five basic offerings, the trespass offering is not very important and rather easy to understand. Actually, the trespass offering is extremely important and is difficult to understand adequately. Therefore, in our study of Leviticus, we need to read 5:1-10 carefully and attentively.

In talking about sin, many people do not realize that there is a great difference between sin and sins. Sin is a matter of indwelling sin as the nature of Satan within us. Sins are a matter of outward sinful deeds. The sin offering deals with sin, and the trespass offering deals with sins, transgressions, and trespasses, including lies, mistakes, and all kinds of wrongdoing. Trespasses are transgressions, and transgressions are different kinds of sins.

I. THE SIGNIFICANCE
OF THE TRESPASS OFFERING

We first need to see the significance of the trespass offering.

A. The Difference between the Sin
Offering and the Trespass Offering

There is an important difference between the sin offering and the trespass offering. The sin offering signifies Christ as our offering resolving sin in our fallen nature (Rom. 8:3; 2 Cor. 5:21). The trespass offering

signifies Christ as our offering resolving the problem of
sins in our conduct (1 Pet. 2:24; Isa. 53:5-6, 10-11 in ASV).

Romans 8:3 says, "God sending His own Son in the
likeness of the flesh of sin and concerning sin, condemned
sin in the flesh." God has condemned sin. How did He do
this? He did it by sending His own Son in the likeness of
the flesh of sin.

The phrase "likeness of the flesh of sin" combines sin
and the flesh. Our flesh today is the flesh of sin. As we
have pointed out, sin and the flesh are related to Satan, the
world, and the prince of the world. Whereas our flesh is the
flesh of sin, Christ came only in the *likeness* of the flesh of
sin. In Him there was no sin; He did not have sin in His
human nature. Nevertheless, in appearance He bore the
likeness of the flesh of sin.

The flesh of fallen mankind is the flesh of sin. In other
words, the flesh of the fallen human race is one with sin.
Where the flesh is, there is sin. The word *flesh* signifies a
fallen person, and every fallen person is sin. Whether we
love others or hate them, we are sin. Genesis 6:3 says that
fallen man became flesh. Since man has become flesh and
the flesh is of sin, the flesh and sin are one. They are
identical. As fallen human beings, we are flesh, and the
flesh is sin.

God condemned sin by sending His Son in the likeness
of the flesh of sin. When the Lord Jesus was on the cross,
He was sin in the eyes of God. Christ was crucified in His
flesh. This means that His flesh was crucified. Since His
flesh was crucified, sin was condemned because sin and
the flesh are identical. God judged the flesh, and He judged
sin. He did this by judging Jesus on the cross. When God
judged Jesus, He judged the flesh and sin. Moreover, at
that time God destroyed Satan in the flesh, judged the
world that was hanging on Satan, and condemned the
prince of the world and the power struggle. One was
crucified, but five things were dealt with: sin, the flesh,
Satan, the world, and the power struggle. These five things
are one.

Second Corinthians 5:21 says, "Him who did not know

sin He made sin on our behalf." The Lord Jesus did not know sin, but God made Him sin on the cross for our sake. When the Lord Jesus was on the cross, He was not only a sinful person in likeness, even as the brass serpent was a serpent in form (John 3:14), but He was also made sin by God. If Jesus had not been made sin, sin could not have been judged when He was crucified. Sin was condemned because Christ, while He was on the cross, was made sin on our behalf by God.

Whereas the sin offering deals with the sin in our nature inwardly, the trespass offering deals with the sins in our conduct outwardly (1 Pet. 2:24). As the marginal notes in the American Standard Version indicate, Isaiah 53:10 puts the trespass offering together with the sin offering. The same thing is true of chapter five of Leviticus.

B. The Trespass Offering
Eventually Becoming the Sin Offering

The trespass offering eventually becomes the sin offering (Lev. 5:6-8, 11-12). This signifies that Christ's redemption for our sin resolves the problem of sin in its two aspects—sin in our inward nature and sins in our outward conduct. These two aspects of sin make up the totality of sin. John 1:29 speaks of this totality: "Behold, the Lamb of God who takes away the sin of the world!" Although the word *sin* is in the singular, it does not refer merely to the sin in our nature; it denotes the totality of sin, comprising both inward sin and outward sins.

II. A FEMALE FROM THE FLOCK, A SHEEP OR A GOAT, TWO TURTLEDOVES OR TWO YOUNG PIGEONS, OR THE TENTH PART OF AN EPHAH OF FINE FLOUR FOR THE TRESPASS OFFERING

Leviticus 5:5-7 and 11 tell us that the trespass offering may be a female from the flock, a sheep or a goat, two turtledoves or two young pigeons, or the tenth part of an ephah of fine flour. This signifies that the trespass offering for our outward sins, for which even a little fine flour is sufficient, is lighter than the sin offering, which needs a bull, or at least a lamb (4:4, 32).

III. TWO TURTLEDOVES
OR TWO YOUNG PIGEONS, ONE
FOR A SIN OFFERING AND THE OTHER
FOR A BURNT OFFERING,
FORMING A TRESPASS OFFERING

Leviticus 5:7 says, "But if he cannot afford a sheep, then he shall bring his trespass offering to Jehovah for that in which he has sinned, two turtledoves or two young pigeons, one for a sin offering and the other for a burnt offering." Here we see that two turtledoves or two young pigeons, one for a sin offering and the other for a burnt offering, form the trespass offering. This signifies that a trespass is out of the inward sin and out of not living for God. The inward sin needs the sin offering. Not living for God needs the burnt offering. The two are a complete type of Christ as the trespass offering resolving our sins.

In 5:7 we can see the source of a trespass and also the reason for a trespass. From where does a trespass come? What is its source? The source of every trespass is the sin that is in our flesh. What is the reason for a trespass? The reason is our not living for God. Therefore, concerning trespasses we have a source with a reason.

We may say that the inward sin is like a man, a husband, and that not living for God is like a woman, a wife. The marriage of these two produces a child, and the name of the child is trespass.

We may also use a fruit tree to illustrate inward sin, not being for God, and trespasses. A fruit tree needs a proper atmosphere and environment in which to grow. When a fruit tree grows in such an atmosphere and environment, fruit is produced. In this illustration the inward sin is the fruit tree, not loving God and not living for Him make up the atmosphere and environment in which the tree grows, and trespasses and transgressions are the fruit.

Why do we make mistakes and do things that are wrong? We spontaneously and even unintentionally do such things because we have sin in our flesh and because we are not for God and do not love Him and live for Him. If we are for God, we will be sincere, faithful, and careful. This can be proved by our experience. Whenever we are not for God, we become loose, and we may reason, murmur, and criticize others. In Philippians 2:12-14 Paul charges us to work out our own salvation with fear and trembling, doing all things without murmurings and reasonings. When we are for God, we do not murmur, reason, criticize, gossip, or debate. When we are not for God, we are careless in talking about others. But when we are for God, we are very careful about what we say.

The reason for our mistakes and transgressions is our not living for God. Because we are fallen, we are not for God absolutely. Since we were created by God, we should be absolutely for God, yet we are not. We may be for God to a great degree, but we are not for Him absolutely. Our not being absolutely for God indicates that we are still in a fallen situation. We are fallen, a fallen person is flesh, and this flesh is sin, which produces trespasses as the children, as the fruit.

According to 5:7, we need both the sin offering and the trespass offering. The sin offering takes care of the source; the trespass offering takes care of the "children," or the "fruits," produced from this source. From this we see that God is concerned about the source—the sin within us—and also about the fruit which is produced from this source— the outward trespasses. Therefore, we need both the sin offering and the trespass offering.

These two offerings actually deal with one thing—sin. Sin includes both indwelling sin and outward sins. In other words, it is a matter of sin in its totality. As we have pointed out, this is the meaning of the word *sin* in John 1:29. The Lord Jesus, the Lamb of God, has dealt with sin in its totality. On the cross, He was the sin offering and also the trespass offering.

Leviticus 5:1-3 mentions some particular transgressions. Verse 1 says, "When a person sins in that he hears a public charge to testify, and he is a witness, either he has seen or

known the matter, and he does not declare it, then he shall
bear his iniquity." The Hebrew expression translated
"public charge to testify" literally means the "voice of an
oath." "Bear his iniquity" means to bear the responsibility
of sin or guilt. This verse refers to a person who hears a
public charge to testify and does not declare what he
knows and thus must bear his iniquity.

We may think that what is spoken of here is insignificant and that it has nothing to do with us today. However,
this seemingly unimportant matter exposes where we are;
it shows that we are not absolutely for God. If we are really
for God and live for Him, especially in the church life, we
will be faithful, honest, and sincere to testify what we
know. We will testify of the truth. To fail in this matter is to
be dishonest and unfaithful; it is to be unlike our God, who
is faithful and honest.

Leviticus 5:2 goes on to say, "Or when a person touches
any unclean thing, whether the carcass of an unclean
beast, or the carcass of unclean cattle, or the carcass of an
unclean creeping thing, and it is hidden from him and he
is unclean, then he is guilty." Here we see that if a person
does nothing more than touch a carcass, he is unclean, for
he has touched the uncleanness of death. This is a type
that has a spiritual application to us. There is a great deal
of death among the children of God today, and this death
is spreading. Moreover, there are different kinds of death,
signified by the carcasses of unclean beasts, cattle, and
creeping things. The words "it is hidden from him"
indicate that we may not be aware that we have touched
the uncleanness of spiritual death. But if we are enlightened
by the Lord, we will realize how much we have touched the
uncleanness of spiritual death and have been defiled by it.

Leviticus 5:3 continues, "Or when he touches the
uncleanness of man, whatever his uncleanness is whereby
he is unclean, and it is hidden from him, when he knows it,
then he is guilty." The uncleanness of man here signifies
the natural man, the natural life. With the natural man
there is uncleanness. Everything that is discharged from
the natural man and the natural life is unclean.

In our contact with one another as members of the Body, there may be uncleanness—the uncleanness of spiritual death and the uncleanness of the natural being. As we are fellowshipping with one another, we need to be aware of these two kinds of uncleanness. For example, a brother may speak a loving word to you, or he may speak a word of appreciation and respect, but his word is altogether natural. If you take that word, you will be defiled, for you will touch the uncleanness of man, the uncleanness of the natural being.

One day, as I was having fellowship with Brother Nee, he told me that politeness is a kind of leprosy. Being polite is different from being nice. For the sake of a proper human living, we should always be nice to others. To be polite is actually to put on a mask. This means that politeness is a matter of pretending. For instance, one brother may be polite with another brother and then gossip with others about him and criticize him. This is leprosy, something that is even worse than being natural.

The word in Leviticus 5 was spoken not to individuals but to the congregation of God's people. In typology this word is spoken to the church. Among the saints in the church, there may be different kinds of death. Death often spreads among the saints. We may not realize how much we have touched the uncleanness of spiritual death. The spreading of gossip and criticism is the spreading of spiritual death. We may touch death day after day without realizing it. Also, the saints may have "buddy-buddy" relationships and love others in a natural way, not in the spirit. This kind of love is natural, fleshly, and unclean.

If we are enlightened by the Lord through this portion of the Word, we will realize that we surely need the trespass offering. The more we are with the Lord and the more we take Him as the burnt offering, the more we will see that we need Him as the trespass offering and as the sin offering. We need the sin offering to deal with indwelling sin as the source and the trespass offering to deal with the "children," the trespasses produced from this source.

IV. THE BLOOD OF THE TRESPASS OFFERING
A. Some of the Blood
Sprinkled on the Wall of the Altar

Some of the blood of the trespass offering was sprinkled on the wall of the altar (5:9a; 7:2). This signifies the sprinkling power of Christ's blood upon sinners (1 Pet. 1:2).

B. The Remainder of the Blood
Squeezed (Drained) Out at the Base of the Altar

The remainder of the blood was squeezed (drained) out at the base of the altar (Lev. 5:9b). This signifies the blood of Christ as the base of God's forgiveness to sinners (Eph. 1:7).

V. NO OIL OR FRANKINCENSE
PUT UPON THE FINE FLOUR AS A SIN OFFERING
FOR THE TRESPASS OFFERING

Leviticus 5:11 tells us that the one who brings "the tenth part of an ephah of fine flour for a sin offering" is not to "place oil upon it nor put frankincense on it, for it is a sin offering." This signifies that the Holy Spirit and the fragrance of Christ's resurrection are not involved with sin.

LIFE-STUDY OF LEVITICUS

PART ONE — MESSAGE TWENTY-TWO

THE TRESPASS OFFERING
CHRIST FOR THE SINS OF GOD'S PEOPLE

(2)

Scripture Reading: Lev. 5:1—6:7; 7:2

The word in Leviticus 5 was spoken not to an individual saint but to God's congregation, to God's people as an assembly. This word was not given to help and instruct an individual saint. Rather, this word was given for the purpose of keeping God's chosen people, as a body, proper, holy, and separated to Him. Furthermore, what is spoken here should not be applied to secular, human society. God does not have the intention to make the entire human society a congregation like the children of Israel in ancient times. God's intention in Leviticus was to keep His chosen people clean and holy that He might dwell among them. The tabernacle was in the midst of the people, and God wanted the people, who were around the tabernacle, to be holy. This was the reason the word in Leviticus was given.

Let us now consider chapter five of Leviticus verse by verse.

In typology, every aspect of Leviticus 5 has a spiritual significance. Verse 1 says, "When a person sins in that he hears a public charge to testify, and he is a witness, either he has seen or known the matter, and he does not declare it, then he shall bear his iniquity." This verse actually deals with lying. A lie involves Satan, for he is the father of lies (John 8:44).

Leviticus 5:2 says, "When a person touches any unclean thing, whether the carcass of an unclean beast, or the carcass of unclean cattle, or the carcass of an unclean creeping thing, and it is hidden from him and he is unclean, then he is guilty." This verse speaks of the carcasses of beasts, cattle, and creeping things. The beasts are wild animals, and the cattle are domesticated animals. According to chapter eleven, the animals in this verse typify different kinds of people. Some people are like beasts, others are like cattle, and still others are like creeping things. The word *carcass* in 5:2 signifies death. The carcasses of these three kinds of animals—the carcass of beasts, the carcass of cattle, and the carcass of creeping things—thus signify three kinds of death. One kind of death is wild like a wild beast. A second kind of death is mild like a gentle, domesticated animal. A third kind of death is subtle like a creeping thing. In typology this indicates that among God's people there may be three kinds of death: wild death, mild death, and subtle death.

Among God's people, that is, in the church life, there may not only be death; there may be different kinds of death. Death may spread among us in a wild way, in a mild way, or in a subtle way. During my years in the church life, I have seen these three kinds of death. I have seen the kind of death that is wild and the kind of death that is mild and gentle. I have also seen the kind of death that creeps in in a subtle, cunning way. Have you not experienced some kind of death in the church life? Perhaps you have experienced the kind of death that is typified by the carcass of a creeping thing, the death that comes in to spread its poison secretly and subtly.

Regardless of its kind, death is death, and it is unclean. Every kind of death—wild, mild, and subtle—is filthy and defiling. It is not easy in the church life to stay away from the uncleanness of these different kinds of death.

According to the typology in the Old Testament, sin is not as dirty as death. If one sinned, he could be forgiven and cleansed immediately by offering a trespass offering (5:10). But if one touched death, he had to wait a few days to become clean. From this we can see that death is more defiling than sin. However, we in the church life may think that sin is serious but that touching death is common and not serious. But in the eyes of God to touch death is the most serious thing.

The poison of death can damage and destroy the saints. In Romans 14 Paul says that we should not destroy the work of God by doing things carelessly (vv. 15, 20). Christ has redeemed and saved the saints, and we should not destroy them by acting carelessly. The Lord has done a lot of gracious, redemptive work on the saints in the Lord's recovery, and for years we have been working to build up the saints. No one should destroy the gracious work of Christ on the saints. No one should destroy those on whom we have been working for their building up. Would not our hearts be hurt to see the saints destroyed by the poison of death? We need to be sober, fair, calm, and kind to consider whether we are really building up the Body of Christ or unconsciously doing something to destroy God's work by spreading the poison of death.

Leviticus 5:3 says, "When he touches the uncleanness of man, whatever his uncleanness is whereby he is unclean, and it is hidden from him, when he knows it, then he is guilty." The "uncleanness of man" here signifies the uncleanness of man's natural life. The Lord Jesus said that nothing that goes into us defiles us; rather, what comes out of us defiles us (Matt. 15:17-20). The natural life, like death, brings in uncleanness. In the church life, in the holy community, death and the natural life may be prevailing.

The natural life includes the matter of natural affection. Either we do not care for one another or we love one another in a natural way, in the way of natural affection. Someone may have had an affection for you in the past, but today he does not care for you at all. This is not according to our Christian nature to love, help, and take care of others. It is altogether in the natural realm. We may love others or, seeking vain glory and being jealous of others, we may envy them. This love and this envy are both of the natural life.

Leviticus 5:4 continues, "Or when a person utters an oath, speaking rashly with his lips to do evil or to do good, in whatever a man may speak rashly with an oath, and it is hidden from him, when he knows it, then he is guilty in any of these." Here we have the matter of speaking rashly, of speaking something before God in a hasty, careless, and reckless way. We may hear about a certain thing and immediately say that we like it or do not like it and that we will do this or that concerning it. To speak in such a way indicates not merely that we do not live for God but that we do not even fear God. Who are we to say rashly that we do not like a certain thing? God may like it. We are not God, and we need to be careful about speaking hastily. Instead of expressing our opinion about a matter, we should say nothing and, if necessary, bring the matter to the Lord, praying and asking Him to show us whether we should have a share in it or stay away from it. This is the right attitude of a person who fears God.

In 5:1-4 we have four items as illustrations of things which need the trespass offering. If we were to make a list of such things, we would not list the four items mentioned here: not witnessing what we know (v. 1), touching the carcass of an animal (v. 2), touching the uncleanness of man (v. 3), and speaking rashly (v. 4). God speaks of these items, for He knows the real situation and need of His people.

The first item, not witnessing what we know, is actually a matter of lying. As we have pointed out, this involves Satan, the father of lies. Therefore, Satan is alluded to here.

The second item is death in three forms—wild, mild, and subtle. Death is the most hateful thing in the eyes of God. Death is spread in a wild way, in a gentle way, and in a subtle way. This is the real situation among God's congregation in this age.

The third item is the natural life with its uncleanness. It is very common for Christians to walk and act in the natural life. Is the natural life not prevailing in today's church life? Those who are sociable in a natural way are often well received, but those who walk in the spirit are often misunderstood. A great deal of the natural life can be seen among Christians and in God's congregation today.

The fourth item is rash speaking. Those who speak rashly are quick to say whether or not they like a certain thing. These four things are listed by God as sins, and, as such, they need the trespass offering.

Leviticus 5:5 and 6 say, "And it shall be when he is guilty in any of these, then he shall confess that in which he has sinned; and he shall bring his trespass offering to Jehovah for his sin which he has committed, a female from the flock, a sheep or a goat for a sin offering; and the priest shall make propitiation for him concerning his sin." The largest trespass offering is a sheep or a goat. This trespass offering reminds us mainly of one thing: that our sins issue from the sin that dwells in us. Apparently we are dealing with sins; actually we are dealing with sin as the source of our sins. For this reason the trespass offering is a sin offering. We realize that we have committed sins, but in the eyes of God these sins have their source in sin. Therefore, what we offer to God to deal with our sins eventually is not merely a trespass offering but is a sin offering.

We may wonder how a trespass offering can become a sin offering. What we bring to God to deal with our sins is a trespass offering. But after we bring this offering to God, it becomes a sin offering. The reason for this is that God will not propitiate us only for our sins; He will propitiate us also for our sin. His way is not merely to remove the fruit from the tree but also to uproot the tree. If the tree is uprooted, the fruit will be thoroughly dealt with. Our problem is not only the sins we have committed; our problem is also the indwelling sin. What we offer to God should deal with sin as well as sins. Therefore, God calls this trespass offering a sin offering.

Verse 7 goes on to say, "But if he cannot afford a sheep, then he shall bring his trespass offering to Jehovah for that in which he has sinned, two turtledoves or two young pigeons, one for a sin offering and the other for a burnt offering." This verse reveals that the trespass offering is related not only to the sin offering but also to the burnt offering. According to this verse, the trespass offering is composed of the sin offering and the burnt offering. Put together, these two offerings constitute the trespass offering.

We may think that our only problem is the sins we have committed. Actually our real problem is the indwelling sin and our not living for God. The root, the source, of our sins is our sin, and the reason for our sins is that we are not absolute for God. Therefore, we not only need the trespass offering to deal with our sins; we also need the sin offering to deal with the root of our sins—the sin within us—and the burnt offering to deal with the reason for our sins—our not being absolute for God. If we deal with the source of our sins and with our not being absolute for God, we also deal with our trespasses.

Verses 8 and 9 continue, "He shall bring them to the priest, who shall offer the one for the sin offering first; he shall nip its head at the neck, but shall not sever it; and he shall sprinkle some of the blood of the sin offering on the wall of the altar, and the remainder of the blood shall be squeezed out at the base of the altar; it is a sin offering." These verses speak not of the trespass offering but of the sin offering and the blood of the sin offering. Some of the blood is sprinkled on the wall of the altar, signifying the sprinkling of Christ's blood upon sinners (1 Pet. 1:2). The remainder of the blood is squeezed out at the base of the altar, signifying that the blood of Christ is the base of God's forgiveness to sinners (Eph. 1:7).

Verse 10 speaks of the second bird. "The second bird he shall then prepare as a burnt offering according to the ordinance. Thus the priest shall make propitiation for him concerning his sin which he has sinned, and he shall be forgiven." According to the regulations, we should be absolute for God. Since we are not absolute for God, we need the burnt offering in addition to the sin offering.

VI. A HANDFUL OF FINE FLOUR
BURNED ON THE ALTAR,
AS AN OFFERING OF JEHOVAH BY FIRE

Verse 11 tells us, "But if he cannot afford two turtledoves or two young pigeons, then he shall bring his

offering for that in which he has sinned, the tenth part of
an ephah of fine flour for a sin offering; he shall not place
oil upon it nor put frankincense on it, for it is a sin
offering." A handful of fine flour burned on the altar, as an
offering of Jehovah by fire, indicates that the fine flour for
the trespass offering for God to forgive our sins is based
upon the shedding of blood on the altar (Heb. 9:22), and it
signifies that the perfect Christ is our trespass offering
based upon the shedding of His blood on the cross (Col.
1:20).

For propitiation there is the need of the shedding of
blood, but in Leviticus 5:11 fine flour is used for a sin
offering. This fine flour typifies the humanity of Jesus.
Thus, the trespass offering not only includes the sin
offering and the burnt offering, but it even refers to the
humanity of Jesus.

We commit many sins not only because we have sin
within us and not only because we are not absolute for
God, but also because we do not have the humanity of
Jesus. Jesus would never commit sins. He has no sin in
Him, and He is absolute for God. His humanity has no part
with the father of lies. His humanity would never touch
anything of death or of the natural life. Furthermore, His
humanity would never do or speak anything rashly,
hastily, or recklessly. Rather, as John 7:3-8 illustrates,
when He was on earth, He always spoke and acted with
consideration.

Why do we have sin in us? Why are we not absolute for
God? The reason we have sin in us and are not absolute for
God is that we are lacking the humanity of Jesus.

The tenth part of an ephah of fine flour offered for a sin
offering signifies that only a small portion of the humanity
of Jesus is needed. This indicates how little we use the
Lord's humanity. We are what we are because we are short
of the Lord's humanity. Due to this shortage, we are full of
lies, death, the natural life, and rashness. However, the
humanity of Jesus is an all-inclusive dose to kill our germs,
to heal our disease, and to supply our need. I believe that
there would be a great change in our married life and in

our relationship with the brothers and sisters in the church
life if we had more of the humanity of Jesus.

VII. THE REMAINDER OF THE FINE
FLOUR FOR THE TRESPASS OFFERING
BEING THE PRIEST'S, LIKE THE MEAL OFFERING

Leviticus 5:13 says, "Thus the priest shall make
propitiation for him concerning his sin which he has
committed in any of these things, and he shall be forgiven;
and the remainder shall be the priest's, like the meal
offering." The remainder of the fine flour for the trespass
offering being the priest's signifies that the redeeming
Christ is the serving one's food.

VIII. A PERSON SINNING
AGAINST THE HOLY THINGS OF JEHOVAH,
AGAINST JEHOVAH, AND LYING TO,
EXTORTING FROM, OR SWEARING FALSELY
TO HIS FELLOW MAN

Leviticus 5:15, 17-18; 6:2-3, 6 speak of a person sinning
against the holy things of Jehovah, or sinning, making
error, against Jehovah, or a person sinning and acting
unfaithfully against Jehovah, and lying to his fellow man
in regard to a deposit or a security, or through robbery, or
extorting from his fellow man, or finding what was lost
and lying about it, and swearing falsely. Such a person
needs a ram without blemish out of the flock, according to
the valuation by the shekel of the sanctuary, for a trespass
offering. This signifies that the Christ who is without sin
and who measures up to the divine scale is qualified to be
the trespass offering for our sins against the holy things of
God, or against God, or against man in the above-listed
trespasses.

IX. THE ONE SINNING AGAINST THE HOLY
THINGS OF GOD AND THE ONE SINNING
AGAINST MAN NEEDING TO MAKE RESTITUTION

The one sinning against the holy things of God needs to
make restitution and add to it one-fifth more and give it to
the priest (5:15-16). Likewise, the one sinning against man

in any defrauding needs to make restitution for it in full, add to it one-fifth more, and give it to whom it belongs on the day he is found guilty (6:2-6). This signifies that the one offering the trespass offering should be righteous in material things according to the divine scale, standard, and measurement.

X. THE TRESPASS OFFERING BEING SLAUGHTERED WHERE THE BURNT OFFERING IS SLAUGHTERED

"In the place where they slaughter the burnt offering they shall slaughter the trespass offering" (7:2a). The trespass offering being slaughtered where the burnt offering is slaughtered indicates that the trespass offering is based upon the burnt offering, and it signifies that Christ is the trespass offering for us based upon His being the burnt offering.

The trespass offering is not simple. It includes dealing with the indwelling sin and with not being absolute for God. It also includes the liar Satan, the death among God's congregation, the natural life with its uncleanness, and the presumption of doing things rashly before God without fear and consideration. Furthermore, the trespass offering includes robbing and defrauding our fellow man.

How can we experience the trespass offering? The experience of the trespass offering is the result of our enjoyment of Christ as the burnt offering, the meal offering, the peace offering, and the sin offering in the fellowship of God and in the divine light. The experience of the trespass offering is therefore the issue of the enjoyment of the Triune God. Our experience of the trespass offering implies our being absolute for God and our knowing that we have sin within us as the source of all kinds of trespasses toward God and man.

LIFE-STUDY OF LEVITICUS

THE LAW OF THE BURNT OFFERING

Scripture Reading: Lev. 6:8-13

Beginning with this message, we will cover the laws of the offerings. The laws of the offerings are the ordinances and regulations of the offerings. For each offering there is a law, a regulation, an ordinance. The laws of the offerings appear to be quite simple. Actually, as we will see, something of deep and high spiritual significance is hidden in these laws.

I. THE BURNT OFFERING
BEING UPON THE HEARTH (FIREWOOD)
ON THE ALTAR ALL NIGHT UNTIL THE MORNING

A. Signifying That Anything
Offered as a Burnt Offering Must Be
Put on the Place of Burning to Be Burned

Leviticus 6:9a says, "Command Aaron and his sons and say, This is the law of the burnt offering: the burnt offering itself shall be upon the hearth on the altar all night until the morning." This signifies that anything offered as a burnt offering must be put on the place of offering to be burned. This is something that worldly people cannot understand, for they are raised and educated to become something in the world. Worldly parents certainly do not teach their children to offer themselves to God to be burned.

By the Lord's mercy and grace, our heart is different from the heart of the unbelievers. We know that the burnt offering indicates that we have a heart that is absolute for God in this age. We are not for anything else, and we have no other interest. Even though we encourage the young people to get the best education, education is not the thing we love. The young people may get the highest education, but they need to realize that on this earth we Christians will eventually be nothing but ashes. This will be the issue of our offering ourselves to God as a burnt offering and of our being burned.

I would like to say a word to the young people who have the heart to serve the Lord full-time. I must tell you that hardships await you and that there is no future for you on earth. You will have nothing earthly on which to rely for your security and for your human living. You may feel that you will be very useful to God, but in the end you will be ashes. Everyone wants to be somebody, but if you would serve the Lord Jesus full-time, you must prepare yourself to be nobody, even to be ashes. Are you willing to be burned? To be burned to ashes is a matter not of enjoyment but of suffering. The destiny of a full-timer is a life of suffering. What is offered to God as a burnt offering must be on the place of burning, not on the place of anything glorious or high. Eventually, the outcome of such a life, a life of suffering, a life without a future and without security, will be a heap of ashes.

Although we have no earthly security, I can testify that we have the Lord Jesus as our security. Christ is my security, even though He sometimes hides Himself from me in order to test me. As a result of my experience and learning, I can tell you that the best time to enjoy the Lord Jesus is when He is hiding from you. After seeming to disappear for a while, He will spontaneously appear to us again. This is often His way with us. Such a Christ is our real security.

B. What Is Offered
Should Remain at the Burning
Place through the Dark Night until Morning

The burnt offering's being upon the hearth (firewood) on the altar all night until the morning also signifies that what is offered should remain at the burning place through the dark night until morning. "All night" means all this dark age. The age we are in is a dark night. The burnt offering should be burning continually through the whole night until the morning.

No matter how long the night may be, eventually there will be a morning, a sun rising. The real sun rising will be the Lord's coming back, and we are waiting for this. However, we should not expect the Lord Jesus to come back quickly to spare us from the trial of the dark night. The more we ask Him to come quickly for this reason, the more He may delay His coming for our sake and for the sake of our passing through a longer dark night.

Recently I spoke a word to the full-timers in Taipei concerning sufferings and hardships. I told them to be prepared to have a life that will not be easy and to take a way that will not be smooth but rugged. We need to remain on the place of burning and be burned throughout the dark night until morning.

II. THE FIRE ON THE ALTAR BEING KEPT BURNING CONTINUALLY AND NOT GOING OUT

The fire on the altar should be kept burning continually (6:9b, 12a, 13). Verse 12a says, "The fire on the altar shall be kept burning on it; it must not go out."

A. Signifying That God as the Burning Fire in the Universe Is Ready to Receive (Burn) What Is Offered to Him as Food

The continual burning of the fire on the altar first signifies that God as the holy fire in the universe is ready to receive (burn) what is offered to Him as food. God's receiving us is His burning us. When we are burned by God, we should be happy because this burning means that God is receiving us.

B. Signifying That God's Desire to Accept What Is Offered to Him Never Ceases

The continual burning of the fire also signifies that God's desire to accept what is offered to Him never ceases. God desires to accept us, and He accepts us by burning us. The more He burns us, the more He accepts us.

III. THE PRIEST BURNING
WOOD ON THE ALTAR EVERY MORNING

The priest burned wood on the altar every morning
(v. 12b). This signifies the need of the serving one's cooperation with God's desire. This cooperation is to add
more fuel to the holy fire to strengthen the burning for
the receiving of the burnt offering as God's food. As we
are being burned, we need to add more wood to burn
ourselves and also to burn our fellow serving ones. Do
not quench the fire but add more wood to keep the fire
burning.

If there were only one serving one, the burning fuel
would be exhausted. Therefore, we need more serving ones,
more companions in being burned. The more serving ones
there are, the more fuel there will be to burn ourselves and
others.

The priest was to burn wood on the altar every
morning. The morning signifies having a new start for the
burning.

IV. THE PRIEST PUTTING ON
HIS LINEN GARMENT AND LINEN BREECHES
OVER HIS FLESH IN TAKING UP THE ASHES
OF THE BURNT OFFERING

"The priest shall put on his linen garment, putting on
linen breeches over his flesh" (v. 10a). Linen is fine, pure,
and clean. The priest's putting on his linen garment and
linen breeches thus signifies that fineness, purity, and
cleanness are needed in handling the ashes (the result) of
the burnt offering. We should not think of the ashes as
waste that can be handled in a careless manner. On the
contrary, the ashes are the result of the burnt offering, and
in handling this result we need to be proper. We need to be
fine, pure, and clean.

V. THE PRIEST PUTTING ON
OTHER GARMENTS TO CARRY THE ASHES
OUTSIDE THE CAMP

"Then he shall take off his garments and put on other

garments, and carry the ashes outside the camp to a clean place" (v. 11). This signifies the stateliness in handling the ashes (the result) of the burnt offering. In God's eyes, the result of our burnt offering is highly regarded. It is fine, pure, and clean. Thus, in carrying the ashes outside the camp, the priest wore stately garments and carried the ashes in a stately way. This teaches us to have a high regard for the result of our burnt offering.

To become a full-timer is to offer ourselves to God as a burnt offering. Concerning this, there should be and must be a result. We should regard this result and not despise it or consider it insignificant. The result of our being a burnt offering will be something that carries out God's New Testament economy. What we do as full-timers is not merely to preach the gospel to save sinners, to establish local churches, to teach the Bible, or to help people to grow in life and in truth. What we do must result in the building up of the Body of Christ, which is a miniature of the coming New Jerusalem.

What we are doing is actually extraordinary, but to the worldly people it is nothing. To them what we are doing is ashes. However, God has a high regard for these ashes. Eventually these ashes will become the New Jerusalem. Have you ever realized that the ashes, the result of the burnt offering, will be the coming New Jerusalem? I realize this, and I believe it. I believe that I will be there and that what I am doing will be part of that city. The New Jerusalem is our destiny and our destination.

How can the ashes of the burnt offering become the New Jerusalem? Ashes indicate the result of Christ's death, which brings us to an end, that is, to ashes. But Christ's death brings in resurrection. In resurrection, the ashes become precious materials—gold, pearls, and precious stones—for the building of the New Jerusalem. All three precious materials come from the transformation of the ashes. When we are brought to ashes, we are brought into the transformation of the Triune God.

VI. THE PRIEST ARRANGING THE BURNT
OFFERING ON THE ALTAR AND BURNING
THE FAT PORTIONS OF THE PEACE OFFERING ON IT

"The priest shall...arrange the burnt offering on it; and he shall offer up in smoke the fat portions of the peace offerings on it" (6:12b). This indicates that to burn the burnt offering is to lay the foundation for the sweetness of the peace offering. The burnt offering is therefore for the enjoyment of the peace offering. In its spiritual significance, the peace offering implies fellowship with the Triune God and includes the enjoyment of the Triune God. The burnt offering was burned, but it was burned for the peace offering.

A. Signifying That We Should
Have the Burning of Our Burnt Offering Laid
as a Foundation for Our Sweet Fellowship with God

The burning of the fat portions of the peace offerings in 6:12 signifies that we should have the burning of our burnt offering laid as a foundation for our sweet fellowship with God. Regardless of how much we feel that we are enjoying Christ, if we do not have the real offering of the burnt offering, our enjoyment is in self-deceit. The real enjoyment of the Lord is based on our offering ourselves to God as a burnt offering. If we mean business with God and offer ourselves to Him and live a life that is absolute for Him, then our enjoyment of Christ will be real and not imaginary.

We should not deceive ourselves but consider whether we have the necessary foundation for us to enjoy the Triune God. This is not a matter of how we feel; it is a matter of actually having a proper foundation for the enjoyment of Christ. We lay this foundation by offering ourselves to the Lord as a burnt offering, and therefore we are willing to be absolute for the Lord, and we actually are absolute for Him. If we have such a foundation, then, whether we feel like we are enjoying the Lord or not, we are enjoying Him in reality. However, if we live a loose life day by day, yet feel that we are enjoying the Lord, we deceive ourselves, because our enjoyment has no foundation. Our need to have a foundation for the enjoyment of Christ is clearly pictured here in the type.

B. Signifying That on the Foundation of the Burnt Offering Our Peace Offering Should Be Burned for a Fragrance to God

Leviticus 6:12b also signifies that on the foundation of the burnt offering our peace offering should be burned for a fragrance to God. Not only the foundation should be burned, but even the very peace, the very fellowship, we enjoy should also be burned. The burnt offering should be burned, and our peace offering also should be burned. This means that both our absoluteness for God and our enjoyment of the Triune God should be a matter of burning. Thus, there is burning upon burning.

In this message we have seen the regulations concerning the burnt offering. If we desire to offer Christ as our burnt offering, taking Him as our burnt offering and enjoying Him as our absoluteness toward God, we need to follow all these regulations.

LIFE-STUDY OF LEVITICUS

PART ONE — MESSAGE TWENTY-FOUR

THE LAW OF THE MEAL OFFERING

Scripture Reading: Lev. 6:14-23

The meal offering is not common food for common people. The meal offering is food only for the priests. All New Testament believers are priests. Thus, the meal offering is for those in the church life who are God's actual and practical priests today.

I. THE MEAL OFFERING TO BE OFFERED BEFORE JEHOVAH IN FRONT OF THE ALTAR

Leviticus 6:14 says, "This is the law of the meal offering: the sons of Aaron shall offer it before Jehovah in front of the altar." The meal offering being offered before Jehovah signifies that the meal offering is offered to God in His presence. The meal offering being offered in front of the altar signifies that the meal offering is offered in relation to the redemption of Christ on the cross. The altar is a type of the cross. In the Old Testament there is the altar, but in the New Testament there is the cross. "In front of the altar" therefore means in relation to the redemption of Christ on the cross. The meal offering is offered to God in His presence, but it must be offered in relation to the redemption of Christ on the cross.

II. THE PORTION OF THE MEAL OFFERING TO AARON AND HIS SONS TO BE EATEN IN A HOLY PLACE, IN THE COURT OF THE TENT OF MEETING

Leviticus 6:16 says, "The remainder of it Aaron and his sons shall eat; it shall be eaten unleavened in a holy place; they shall eat it in the court of the tent of meeting." This verse speaks of the portion of the meal offering which was for Aaron and his sons, that is, the portion which is for the priests in their priestly service.

A. Signifying That We
Enjoy Christ as Our Meal Offering
(Life Supply for Our Service) without Sin

Eating the priests' portion of the meal offering in a holy place signifies that we enjoy Christ as our meal offering (life supply for our service) without sin. The word *holy* here indicates that the enjoyment of the meal offering must be without sin.

B. Signifying That We Enjoy
Christ in a Separated, Sanctified Realm

Eating the meal offering in a holy place also signifies that we enjoy Christ in a separated, sanctified realm. We can take Christ as our meal offering, as our daily life supply, only in a holy place. A holy place is a sanctified realm.

C. Signifying That We Enjoy
Christ in the Sphere of the Church

The priests' portion of the meal offering was eaten in the court of the tent of meeting. The tent of meeting typifies the church. Therefore, eating the meal offering in the court of the tent of meeting signifies enjoying Christ in the sphere of the church. Outside the sphere of the church, there is no meal offering for us. The meal offering can be applied only in the sphere of the church life. We can enjoy Christ as our meal offering for our priestly service only within the circle of the church life. Our enjoyment of Christ as the meal offering must be holy, it must be in a sanctified realm, and it must be in the sphere of the church life.

Christ is our meal offering that we may serve God as priests. However, many real believers today are priests of God in name but not in actuality. In their daily life, they are not priests of God.

To be a priest one does not need to be a full-timer. We became priests by our regeneration. Having been regenerated, we should now live a life as God's priests, serving God. You may serve God as a priest even though you have a full-time job. We may be engaged in different kinds of proper employment, but we can still do our work in the sense of being priests to God. For example, a brother who is a physician may carry out his medical practice as a priestly service, preaching the gospel to unbelievers to bring them to Christ and ministering life to believers. If we all behaved as priests in this way, serving God in His gospel, in His mercy, in His grace, and in His life, this would be the best way to preach the gospel.

However, the actual situation among believers is the opposite. More than half of the people in the United States may be Christians, but it is rare to hear of anyone preaching the gospel in their place of employment. Many believers live like worldlings, like common people, not like priests. What a shame! Since we are priests, we need to ask ourselves about our gospel preaching.

According to my study of the New Testament, the first thing we should do as God's priests is to preach the gospel and bring the sinners to God as offerings. This is what Paul did; his preaching of the gospel was a priestly service (Rom. 15:16). In his priestly service he offered the Gentiles to God. Do we have some saved sinners whom we can offer to God?

The book of Leviticus is altogether concerned with the priests. Nearly every chapter concerns the life, living, need, and supply of the priests and all the other things related to them. If we are not priests in actuality, we are not qualified to enter into this book. Therefore, I am deeply burdened to beg you to come back to your heavenly calling as priests of God. The first duty of our priestly service must be to bring sinners to present to God as offerings.

Paul said that he was saved to be an example to all the believers (1 Tim. 1:16). He was the believers' pattern, and his first duty was to gain sinners and offer them to God as offerings. His work of preaching was the real New Testament priestly service. Surely Paul knew what it meant to have Christ as his meal offering for his priestly service. But the meal offering may not be as real to us as it was to Paul, because only to a small degree is our life actually the life of a priest. How sad it would be if we only talked about the priestly service but were not actually in it!

In these days while I am considering the book of Leviticus, my heart is weeping. The more I read and study this book, the more my heart is weeping. Among us there is little that would cause us to be joyful. We are talking about the priestly food, but who are the priests, and where are they? In this message I am burdened to stress this one point—the book of Leviticus is for the priests.

Regarding the priestly service, we need to consider our situation and ask ourselves where we are. The prophet Haggai charged the people of Israel to consider their ways (Hag. 1:5-11). We all need to reconsider our way. What kind of believers are we? Are we priestly believers or common believers?

III. NOT BAKING THE MEAL OFFERING WITH LEAVEN

Speaking of the meal offering, Leviticus 6:17a says, "It shall not be baked with leaven." Not baking the meal offering with leaven signifies that our working on Christ as our life supply must be without sin.

IV. CONSIDERING THE MEAL OFFERING MOST HOLY, LIKE THE SIN OFFERING AND THE TRESPASS OFFERING

The meal offering "is most holy, like the sin offering and like the trespass offering" (v. 17b). Here the meal offering is mentioned in relation to the sin offering and the trespass offering. We should consider all these offerings most holy.

A. Signifying That to Enjoy Christ as the Life Supply We Need to Deal with Sin in Our Fallen Nature

The sin offering deals with sin in our fallen nature. If we would enjoy Christ as our life supply, we need to deal with the sin in us.

B. Signifying That to Enjoy
Christ as the Life Supply We Also
Need to Deal with the Sins in Our Conduct

The trespass offering deals with the sins in our conduct. If we would enjoy Christ as our life supply, we need to deal not only with sin but also with our sins.

When we enjoy Christ as our daily supply for our priestly service, we need to realize that this enjoyment involves dealing with the sin in our fallen nature and also dealing with the sins in our conduct. If we try to enjoy the meal offering without such a dealing, we commit sin. We cannot take Christ as the meal offering unless we deal with our inward sin and our outward sins. This is the reason the meal offering refers us to the sin offering and to the trespass offering.

V. EVERY MALE AMONG THE SONS
OF AARON EATING OF THE MEAL OFFERING

A. Signifying That the Partakers of Christ
as the Life Supply Should Be Strong in Life

"Every male among the sons of Aaron may eat of it; it is their perpetual due throughout your generations from the offerings of Jehovah by fire" (v. 18a). Here we see that every male among the sons of Aaron could eat of the meal offering. This signifies that the partakers of Christ as the life supply should be strong in life.

When we hear that we need to be strong in life to partake of the meal offering, we may be disappointed, feeling that we are disqualified. This is the reason that nearly every day I make a strong petition to the Lord: "Lord, have mercy on us all." Our situation is probably suitable only for the Lord's mercy. Actually, according to this particular statute in the law of the meal offering, we are not qualified to partake of the meal offering. We are not the males among the sons of Aaron; that is, we are not the stronger ones in life among the saints. It is the stronger ones in life who are qualified to enjoy Christ as the meal offering.

No matter how much we may think we have the daily

enjoyment of Christ, we actually have not enjoyed Him that much. Our enjoyment is short because we have a problem in life. We are still so young and feeble in life. We are not the proper males. What we are, God knows, and we also know. We cannot say that we are adequately strong in the divine life. For this reason we need to ask the Lord to have mercy on us all. We need the Lord's mercy.

B. Signifying That the Partakers of Christ Should Be God's Serving Ones—Priests

The males among the sons of Aaron eating of the meal offering also signifies that the partakers of Christ should be God's serving ones—priests. If we do our daily work without serving God as a priest, we cannot share in the real enjoyment of Christ. In such a case, we may think that we have this enjoyment, but our thought does not correspond to the actual situation.

VI. THE MEAL OFFERING OF AARON AND HIS SONS ON THE DAY WHEN AARON IS ANOINTED

"This is the offering of Aaron and his sons which they shall offer to Jehovah on the day when he is anointed" (v. 20a). This signifies that the enjoyment of Christ as the life supply is related to the priestly service. Again and again I would emphasize the fact that the enjoyment of Christ as the meal offering is related to our priestly service.

A. The Tenth of an Ephah of Fine Flour as a Continual Meal Offering

Verse 20b speaks of "the tenth of an ephah of fine flour as a continual meal offering." This signifies that the top portion, the tenth part, of the enjoyment of Christ should be for God. This also signifies that this kind of enjoyment of Christ should continue in our priestly service.

B. Half of the Meal Offering in the Morning and Half in the Evening to Keep It a Continual Offering

Half of the meal offering was offered in the morning

and half in the evening to keep it a continual offering (v. 20c). This signifies the continual enjoyment of Christ in the priestly service.

The meal offering is only for the priests, and it is prevailing only in the priestly service. We may be priests, but our priestly service may not be prevailing. If this is our situation, then the priestly food will likewise not be prevailing. This spiritual food can be prevailing only in a prevailing priestly service. We must be serving priests in actuality. Then the priestly food will actually be our portion.

C. The Meal Offering Being
Entirely Burned and Not Eaten by the Priest

"It is a perpetual statute; it shall be entirely offered up in smoke to Jehovah. Every meal offering of a priest shall be entirely burned; it must not be eaten" (vv. 22b-23). This signifies that the enjoyment of Christ for God's satisfaction should be absolute.

Our enjoyment of Christ is measured by the extent to which we are actually priests serving God. Our feeling is not the measurement. We are priests, but if there is a problem with our priestly service, there will also be a problem with the enjoyment of Christ as the meal offering.

In doing anything, we need to be in the right position. If we are not in the right position, then we cannot have anything to do with that particular matter. Although we are priests, in a practical way we may be in the wrong position and therefore cannot have the real enjoyment of Christ as the meal offering.

My loving intention in speaking this word is to encourage you to reconsider your way. Do not think that you are all right. I can testify to you that daily I need to reconsider my way and my situation. This is a serious matter because none of us knows when the Lord might take him. We may be taken at any time. Once the Lord takes us away, it will be too late for us to do anything about our situation. We have been clearly told that at His coming the Lord will set up a judgment seat (Rom. 14:10;

2 Cor. 5:10). We all will stand there and give an account to Him. In particular, we will have to confess all the words that came out of our mouth while we were on earth (Matt. 12:36-37). Therefore, we need to be careful in what we speak.

My desire is not to be an expositor of the Bible. My burden is to minister the Lord's word in a living and enlightening way. I would like all the dear saints to be enlightened and to see some light concerning themselves, concerning the church, and concerning God's New Testament economy. It is crucial that we be brought into the light and that the light shine upon us, around us, and within us.

We need to remember that the first three offerings—the burnt offering, the meal offering, and the peace offering— bring us into the light. In the light we are enlightened to see our sin and our sins. This is what we need.

Whether we are old or young, whether we have been saved for many years or for a few months, we need to be enlightened. We all need to be brought into the divine light. We thank the Lord that we are children of light (Eph. 5:8). Since we are children of light, we must be in the light to be clear first concerning ourselves and then concerning God's economy. This is what I am expecting to see.

LIFE-STUDY OF LEVITICUS

PART ONE — MESSAGE TWENTY-FIVE

THE LAW OF THE SIN OFFERING

Scripture Reading: Lev. 6:24-30

In this message we will consider the law of the sin offering.

It is not difficult for us to consider as law the Ten Commandments given through Moses. However, we may find it hard to regard as a law something that concerns the enjoyment of Christ. We may think that if there is a law concerning the enjoyment of Christ, there will not be any enjoyment. Nevertheless, each of the five offerings has its own law. Therefore, the sin offering has its law, and with this law there are a number of regulations.

As descendants of Adam we have a fallen life, a lawless life unwilling to be ruled, governed, or controlled by anyone. Our Adamic life is rebellious, and our Adamic nature is lawless. But when we were saved and regenerated, we received another life—the divine life, the life of God—and this life is the opposite of our fallen, lawless life. This means that as genuine believers in Christ, we have two lives, an old one and a new one. The first is the natural, human life, and the second is the divine life, the eternal life. It is not too much to say that the divine life is God Himself; it is God within us to be our life. Whereas the fallen, natural life is lawless, the divine life within us is absolutely according to law and regulation.

Every kind of life has its own law. For example, a bird flies according to the law of the bird life, and a peach tree bears peaches according to the law of the peach tree life. The divine life also has its own law.

The law of the sin offering is according to the law of what we have enjoyed of Christ. In our enjoyment of Christ as the burnt offering, we need to realize that Christ is a life and this life has a law. The law of the burnt offering, therefore, is written according to the law of the Christ whom we have enjoyed. The principle is the same with the other offerings. The peace offering and the meal offering are a living person, Christ. As a living person, Christ has a life with a law. Thus, the law of the peace offering and the law of the meal offering correspond to the life law of Christ. Apparently, the written law concerns only the peace offering and the meal offering. Actually, in our experience, the law of the peace offering and the law of the meal offering become a living law, a law of the very life of the Christ whom we enjoy.

Every law in letters is written according to a certain life. If we were to write a law concerning elderly people, that law would have to correspond to the life of elderly people. The same would be true with a law written concerning young people. This principle applies to the law given to us by God. God has given us a law that we should worship Him because we have a worshipping life. God would never give such a law to animals, because they do not have such a life.

Three portions in the New Testament indicate that even in the enjoyment of Christ we need to be regulated. In 1 Corinthians 9:26 and 27 Paul says, "I therefore so run, not as uncertainly; so I box, not as beating the air; but I buffet my body and lead it as a slave, lest having preached to others, I myself should become disapproved." Literally, the Greek word translated "buffet" means to beat the face under the eye black and blue. This is not to ill-treat the body as in asceticism, nor to consider the body evil as in Gnosticism. This is to subdue the body and make it a conquered captive to serve us as a slave for fulfilling our holy purpose. In these verses we see not only requirements but demands. Here we have the strongest demand of the strongest law.

Galatians 6:15 and 16 say, "Neither is circumcision anything nor uncircumcision, but a new creation. And as many as shall walk by this rule, peace be upon them and mercy, even upon the Israel of God." In verse 15 Paul tells us that "neither is circumcision anything nor uncircumcision, but a new creation." This is grace. Today we do not need circumcision or uncircumcision—we only need grace. But in verse 16 Paul goes on to tell us that the way to receive mercy and peace is to "walk by this rule," the rule of the new creation. God has saved us to the state and condition of a new creation with Christ as its life. Now we need to walk by the rule of this new creation.

The rule of the new creation will regulate us in the time we go to bed at night and rise in the morning. On the Lord's Day in particular, the rule of the new creation will urge us to rise up a little earlier, pray for the meeting, and come to the meeting early to meet with the Lord and worship Him.

The reward for walking according to the rule of the new creation is mercy and peace. I can testify that when I walk according to this rule, I have mercy and peace. If we walk according to the rule of the new creation in the way we prepare for and come to the meeting on the Lord's Day, we will receive mercy and peace.

Walking by the rule of the new creation is a matter of law. In the new creation, there is a new life, and within this new life, there is a new law. This new law is actually the Lord Himself within us, regulating us all the time.

We are God's new creation, and we have the life of this new creation. With this life there is a regulating law. In our daily living, we need to be regulated by this law.

In Philippians 3:13 and 14 Paul tells us that he is forgetting what is behind, stretching forward to what is before, and pursuing "toward the goal for the prize of the high calling of God in Christ Jesus." Then in verses 15 and 16 he says, "Let us therefore, as many as are full-grown, have this mind; and if in anything you are otherwise minded, this also God shall reveal to you. Only this, whereunto we have attained, by the same rule let us

226 LIFE-STUDY OF LEVITICUS

walk." The Greek word translated "walk" here means to walk orderly; it is derived from a word which means to range in regular line, to march in military rank, to keep step, to conform to virtue and piety. Thus, Paul is here charging us to walk in line, in order, and in a regulated way.

These three portions of the New Testament all indicate the same thing—that in the enjoyment of grace we need to be ruled.

I. THE SIN OFFERING
BEING SLAUGHTERED BEFORE JEHOVAH
WHERE THE BURNT OFFERING IS SLAUGHTERED

"Speak to Aaron and to his sons and say, This is the law of the sin offering: in the place where the burnt offering is slaughtered the sin offering shall be slaughtered before Jehovah" (Lev. 6:25a). This signifies two things. First, it signifies that Christ as our sin offering was slain before God. Second, it signifies that Christ was offered to God as our sin offering based upon His being the burnt offering to God.

We may think that if we bring an offering to God, we may slaughter it anywhere. However, here God requires His people to slaughter the sin offering before Him in the place where the burnt offering is slaughtered. The offering must be presented according to God's regulations. From this we see that even though we today are enjoying Christ as grace, there are still regulations that we must follow in the enjoyment of Christ.

II. THE SIN OFFERING BEING MOST HOLY

The sin offering is most holy (6:25b). This signifies that Christ as our sin offering offered to God was most holy in that He dealt with sin in our nature intrinsically and with the whole of our sinful nature. The sin offering deals not only with the sin in our conduct outwardly but also with the sin in our nature intrinsically. This offering deals with the whole of our sinful nature. Therefore, the sin offering is most holy.

III. THE PRIEST OFFERING
THE OFFERING FOR SIN, EATING IT
IN A HOLY PLACE, IN THE COURT
OF THE TENT OF MEETING

A. Signifying That He Who Serves
Sinners with Christ as Their Sin Offering
Shares the Enjoyment of Christ as the Sin Offering

"The priest who offers it for sin shall eat it. In a holy place it shall be eaten, in the court of the tent of meeting" (6:26). This signifies that he who serves sinners with Christ as their sin offering shares the enjoyment of Christ as the sin offering. If we serve sinners with Christ, we are serving as priests. When we minister Christ to others in this way, both we and the ones we are serving will enjoy Christ as the sin offering.

B. Signifying That He Enjoys
Christ as the Sin Offering in a Separated,
Sanctified Realm, in the Sphere of the Church

The priest's eating the sin offering in a holy place, in the court of the tent of meeting, also signifies that he who ministers Christ as the sin offering to sinners enjoys Christ as this offering in a separated, sanctified realm, in the sphere of the church.

We may think that as long as we are serving others with Christ, we can do this anywhere. However, according to the spiritual rule, we must do this according to God's regulation.

IV. WHOEVER TOUCHES
THE FLESH OF THE SIN OFFERING
BEING HOLY

Whoever touched the flesh of the sin offering was holy (6:27a). This signifies that whoever touches Christ as the sin offering is separated and sanctified, forsaking sin and having his natural flesh dealt with, for Christ as the sin offering has dealt with sin and our sinful flesh on the cross.

We need to realize that when we bring Christ as the sin

offering to a sinner, this Christ is holy. When a sinner
touches this holy Christ, he becomes sanctified and is
made holy. Immediately this sanctified one will forsake sin
and have his natural flesh dealt with.

We need to have such a realization and faith concerning
Christ as the sin offering. Then we should bring the
gospel—that is, Christ Himself—to others and let them
touch Him. The Christ whom we minister to others is the
sin offering. On the cross He dealt with the intrinsic sin in
our being and with our sinful flesh.

V. THE GARMENT ON WHICH THE BLOOD
OF THE SIN OFFERING WAS SPATTERED
BEING WASHED IN A HOLY PLACE

"When any of its blood is spattered on a garment, you
shall wash what it was spattered on in a holy place"
(6:27b). This signifies that the daily walk of the one who
has received redemption through the blood of Christ as the
sin offering should be dealt with (cf. Eph. 4:22-24). Our
daily walk, signified by the garment, should be dealt with
continually.

The garment on which the blood of the sin offering was
spattered was washed in a holy place. This signifies that
the daily life of one who has received redemption through
the blood of Christ as the sin offering should be dealt with
in a separated, sanctified realm. From this we see that we
should have regard for the blood of Christ and never
consider it common.

VI. THE EARTHEN VESSEL,
IN WHICH THE SIN OFFERING IS BOILED,
BEING BROKEN

"An earthen vessel in which it is boiled shall be broken"
(6:28a). This signifies that the one who, as an earthen
vessel, has a relationship with Christ as the sin offering
should be broken. To preach Christ to others as the sin
offering, we as the earthen vessels need to be broken. If we
are not broken and yet preach the gospel in our natural
life, we will not see much result. We need to be broken
vessels.

VII. A BRONZE VESSEL,
IN WHICH THE SIN OFFERING IS BOILED,
BEING SCOURED AND RINSED WITH WATER

"If it is boiled in a bronze vessel, then it shall be scoured and rinsed with water" (6:28b). This signifies that the one who has been enlightened and judged by the Spirit (likened to a bronze mirror) to be regenerated needs not to be broken but dealt with by being scoured and rinsed.

If we would go to preach Christ as the sin offering to others, we must be dealt with, either by being broken or by being scoured and rinsed. We cannot go in a natural way.

VIII. EVERY MALE OF THE PRIESTS
EATING OF THE SIN OFFERING, WHICH IS MOST HOLY

"Every male among the priests may eat of it; it is most holy" (6:29). This signifies that all the stronger ones can enjoy Christ as the most holy offering in ministering Christ as the sin offering to sinners.

We should not think that preaching the gospel is a small thing. It requires us to be strong in the life of Christ.

IX. THE SIN OFFERING, THE BLOOD
OF WHICH IS BROUGHT INTO THE TENT OF MEETING
TO MAKE PROPITIATION IN THE HOLY PLACE,
IN THE HOLY OF HOLIES, NOT BEING
EATEN BUT BURNED WITH FIRE

"No sin offering shall be eaten from which any of the blood is brought into the tent of meeting to make propitiation in the holy place; it shall be burned with fire" (6:30). The propitiation mentioned here was made in the Holy of Holies (16:27). This verse signifies that Christ as the sin offering dealing with our sin and with our sinful nature on the cross to accomplish God's redemption for us is wholly for God's enjoyment, and we should not share it. But in our ministering Christ as the sin offering to sinners, we can share Him.

Concerning Christ as the sin offering, there is a portion that is only for God, and there is a portion for us to share. The top portion is for God's enjoyment. God made Christ a propitiation for sinners, and we have no share in this. This is absolutely for God. However, when we preach Christ to others, ministering Him as the sin offering, we can share Him. Thus, God has His part, and we have our part.

These regulations concerning the sin offering are called "the law of the sin offering." This indicates that even in the enjoyment of Christ, we must go along with all the regulations in life. We should not have our own choice in the way to enjoy Christ. We must enjoy Christ in the way chosen by God.

LIFE-STUDY OF LEVITICUS

PART ONE — MESSAGE TWENTY-SIX

THE LAW OF THE TRESPASS OFFERING

Scripture Reading: Lev. 7:1-10

In my study of biographies and history, I have received much help from the living and practices of two persons, George Mueller and Hudson Taylor. George Mueller, a leading one among the British Brethren, rose up every morning to walk in the open air and to read the Bible and pray as he walked. As he read, he prayed. He testified that from this practice he received the best nourishment, edification, knowledge, and building up in his Christian life. The practice of Hudson Taylor, the founder of the China Inland Mission, was very similar. He also rose up in the morning to spend time with the Lord in the Word, and he testified of the nourishment he received.

I mention the practice of George Mueller and Hudson Taylor because I am concerned for the Christian life of the young ones. In the Christian life, spiritual birth is only the beginning. If a human being is to be raised properly and to grow adequately in every phase of life, he must be raised in a good home and attend school from kindergarten through high school. This is the law according to the physical life. The principle is the same in the Christian life. We need a spiritual home where we can grow and a spiritual school where we can receive a proper education. In addition, we need to behave ourselves, cooperating with both the home and the school. This is the law according to the spiritual life.

When we were regenerated, we received another life— the divine life, the life of God—which is different from our natural life. Whether our natural life is good or bad, we need to forget that life and go along with the second life, the divine life. In this second life there is a law that corresponds to the five laws in Leviticus 6 and 7 concerning the enjoyment of Christ in five aspects. Today, we need to go along strictly with this second life. If we do this, we will receive much spiritual benefit.

Every life has its own law and its own sense. The divine life, therefore, has a law and also a sense. To us today, this life is not objective but is altogether subjective. The divine life is in us. This life within us is subjective to such an extent that often we find it difficult to distinguish our original, natural life from our second, divine life. Nevertheless, it is a fact that the divine life is within us, and this life has a particular sense.

Some illustrations will help you understand what I mean by the sense of the divine life within us. Before you were saved, you may have enjoyed a certain kind of worldly entertainment. When you wanted to participate in that kind of entertainment, you simply did so. But after being saved and regenerated, quite often you would have a sense or feeling within that would not agree with your participating in that worldly amusement. You may then have felt that it was better to use the time to pray, and something within you—the sense of the divine life—would agree.

Sometimes the inner sense may not agree with your intention to spend a certain available time in prayer. After further consideration, you may have the desire to visit your cousin to preach the gospel, and the inner sense may agree. Praying and preaching the gospel are both good and holy things; however, the inner sense may agree with the latter and not with the former. Thus, you do not have the peace to stay home and pray, but you do have the peace to preach the gospel. Such an experience tells you that now you have something which you did not have before you were saved— the divine life with its law and its sense or feeling. If you take care of this inner sense, the sense of the divine life, you will keep the law of this life.

I would like to help you to make a decision, to make up your mind, to live and walk according to the law of the new life. You need to decide not to live any longer according to the old way. You are not what you were before you were saved. You are a new creation, a regenerated person, a member of the new man.

Immediately after their regeneration, some believers have not only the desire and the aspiration but even the ambition to be new, holy, heavenly persons. But perhaps some of you have not yet made such a decision. I am concerned that you will continue to live, act, and behave in the old way. Therefore, I would urge you, even beg you, to make a decision that you will not be as you were in the past.

Because we are regenerated persons, we should be different in everything from what we were in the past. We were generated through our parents to receive the natural, human life, but we were regenerated by God to receive the divine life and thereby to become God's children. Now we need to live like children of God.

If you were adopted by the president, surely you would decide spontaneously to live and act like a child of the president. We need to realize that we are children of the Lord of the whole universe, the One who is much higher than the president. Since we are children of such a God, we should behave as His children.

Although we are the children of God, we may come to the meetings of the church in either a proper or an improper way. Some may come to the meeting on the Lord's Day sloppily dressed. They may also come late and take a seat according to their preference. Of course, the meeting is full of grace, and some grace may rain on them, but it is questionable how much grace they will receive and how much they will treasure it. Others may come to the meeting on the Lord's Day properly washed and dressed, and prepared not only in their spirit but also in their whole being. They may even come early, take an appropriate seat, and pray for the meeting. Surely they will receive more grace, and they will treasure what they receive. They will receive spiritual benefit, and they will in turn be a benefit to the church.

We need all kinds of regulations in our Christian life. Some may feel that this is too legal, but here in the type we do have the laws, the regulations, for the enjoyment of Christ.

Let us now consider the various aspects of the law of the trespass offering.

I. THE TRESPASS OFFERING BEING MOST HOLY

"This is the law of the trespass offering; it is most holy" (Lev. 7:1). Like the meal offering and the sin offering, the trespass offering is most holy. This signifies that Christ as our trespass offering is most holy in dealing with the sins in our conduct.

When we apply Christ as our trespass offering, we must do this in a holy way. We should never apply this offering in a loose or careless way, much less in a sinful way. Concerning the trespass offering, we need to remember that God uses this offering to refer us to the sin offering, reminding us that sin is in our flesh and that sin includes Satan, who is the father of lies (John 8:44), the world (1 John 5:19), and the power struggle. The trespass offering also refers us to the burnt offering, reminding us that we commit sins because we are not fully and wholly for God. The reason we lose our temper or strive with certain saints is that we are not wholly for God. Since the trespass offering refers us to the sin offering and the burnt offering, we should not take the trespass offering in a light way. Actually, nearly the entire Christian life is involved with the trespass offering. Therefore, we should have the proper realization of this offering and apply it according to its law.

II. THE TRESPASS OFFERING
BEING SLAUGHTERED IN THE PLACE WHERE
THE BURNT OFFERING IS SLAUGHTERED

"In the place where they slaughter the burnt offering they shall slaughter the trespass offering" (Lev. 7:2a). This signifies that Christ as our trespass offering in dealing with the sins in our conduct is based upon His being the burnt offering to God.

Both the sin offering and the trespass offering are

based on the burnt offering. Because Christ is the burnt offering, He is qualified to be the sin offering and the trespass offering. If Christ were not absolute for God, Christ would not be qualified to be our sin offering and trespass offering. Rather, He Himself would have needed someone to be His sin offering and trespass offering. Being absolute for God is the foundation, the base, for our Savior's being our sin offering and trespass offering. This reminds us and strengthens us when we take Him as our trespass offering to take Him also as our burnt offering so that in Him, with Him, and through Him we may be absolute for God.

III. EVERY MALE OF THE PRIESTS EATING OF THE TRESPASS OFFERING IN A HOLY PLACE

"Every male among the priests may eat of it. It shall be eaten in a holy place; it is most holy" (v. 6). Every male of the priests eating of the trespass offering in a holy place signifies that all the stronger ones can enjoy Christ as the trespass offering in ministering Christ to others in dealing with the sins in their conduct. To minister Christ as the trespass offering to a brother who has committed sins requires that you be a stronger one.

This enjoyment of Christ must be in a holy place, in a separated, sanctified realm. If we would help others to take Christ as their trespass offering for their sins, we must be strong, and we must do this in a realm that is not common or worldly but that is holy and sanctified, separated from all other places.

IV. AS THE SIN OFFERING, SO IS THE TRESPASS OFFERING—ONE LAW FOR BOTH

"As the sin offering, so is the trespass offering; there is one law for them" (v. 7a). This signifies that sin and trespasses (sins) are of the same category. All are sin in its totality. This is the reason the word *sin* in John 1:29 includes sin and sins; that is, it includes the totality of the category of sin.

V. THE PRIEST WHO MAKES PROPITIATION WITH THE TRESPASS OFFERING HAVING IT

"The priest who makes propitiation with it shall have it" (v. 7b). This signifies that the one who ministers with Christ as the trespass offering shares such a Christ. When we minister Christ as the trespass offering to others, we share in Him as this offering. This encourages us to minister Christ.

VI. THE PRIEST WHO OFFERS ANY MAN'S BURNT OFFERING HAVING THE HIDE OF THE BURNT OFFERING

"The priest who offers any man's burnt offering, that priest shall have for himself the hide of the burnt offering which he has offered" (v. 8). This signifies that the one who ministers with Christ as the burnt offering shares and enjoys Christ in His enveloping power.

When we serve others with Christ, we share a particular part of Christ—His "hide," which signifies His enveloping power. To envelop something is to wrap it with some kind of covering, and this covering serves as a protection to that thing. Christ's enveloping power is His covering, protecting, and preserving power. If a cow had no hide, the cow would not be protected and preserved. Today Christ is our covering. He not only covers us but also protects and preserves us and everything related to our being. We experience Christ as our covering, protecting, and preserving power when we minister Him as the burnt offering to others. Because we have a thick hide covering and preserving us, we are protected in every way, and nothing will hurt us.

VII. EVERY MEAL OFFERING BAKED IN THE OVEN OR PREPARED IN A PAN OR ON A GRIDDLE BEING FOR THE PRIEST WHO OFFERS IT

"Every meal offering which is baked in the oven, and any that is prepared in a pan or on a griddle, shall be for the priest himself who offers it" (v. 9). Here we see that these meal offerings with which the priest served eventually became his to enjoy for the priesthood. This signifies that the one who ministers Christ as the suffering One partakes of and enjoys such a Christ. As long as we serve Christ to others, we will have as our enjoyment the very Christ whom we serve.

VIII. EVERY MEAL OFFERING MINGLED WITH OIL OR DRY BEING FOR ALL THE PRIESTS

"But every other meal offering, whether mingled with oil or dry, shall be for all of Aaron's sons, to all alike" (v. 10). This signifies that all those who minister Christ mingled with the Spirit or in Himself alike partake of and enjoy such a Christ.

What we have in these verses is the law of the trespass offering. If we minister Christ to others, we will enjoy Him. This is a law, a regulation, made by God.

LIFE-STUDY OF LEVITICUS

PART ONE — MESSAGE TWENTY-SEVEN

THE LAW OF THE PEACE OFFERING

Scripture Reading: Lev. 7:11-38

The law of the peace offering is a long law concerning
the enjoyment of Christ. No Christian would ever imagine
that the enjoyment of Christ would be so regulated. Both
the Old Testament and the New Testament have warnings
concerning the improper, or lawless, enjoyment of Christ.
First Corinthians 11:17 says that we could meet together
not for the better but for the worse. Verse 27 says,
"Whoever eats the bread or drinks the cup of the Lord in
an unworthy manner shall be guilty of the body and of the
blood of the Lord." Verse 29 speaks of the one who "eats
and drinks judgment to himself, not discerning the body."
Here we see that the word in the New Testament is more
solemn than that in the Old Testament.

Let us now consider a number of points related to the
law of the peace offering.

I. THE PEACE OFFERING
FOR THANKSGIVING BEING OFFERED
WITH THE MEAL OFFERING OF UNLEAVENED CAKES
MINGLED WITH OIL, UNLEAVENED WAFERS
ANOINTED WITH OIL, AND CAKES
OF FINE FLOUR SATURATED, MINGLED WITH OIL

The first kind of peace offering is the peace offering for
thanksgiving. Of all the different peace offerings, this one
is the weakest. Concerning this kind of peace offering,
Leviticus 7:12 says, "If he offers it for thanksgiving, then
with the thanksgiving sacrifice he shall offer unleavened
cakes mingled with oil, and unleavened wafers anointed
with oil, and cakes of fine flour saturated, mingled with
oil." This signifies that Christ, whether mingled with the

Spirit without sin, or anointed with the Spirit without
sin, or as the fine One saturated with the Spirit, as the
meal offering in our enjoyment of Him in His conduct,
is our peace offering, crucified with the shedding of His
blood on the cross (Col. 1:20), in our thanksgiving to
God.

II. WITH THE PEACE OFFERING FOR THANKSGIVING, CAKES OF LEAVENED BREAD BEING OFFERED

"With the thanksgiving sacrifice of his peace offering,
he shall offer his offering with cakes of leavened bread"
(v. 13). This signifies that the offerer, though enjoying
Christ as the One without sin, still has sin.

The reason the peace offering for thanksgiving is the
weakest kind of peace offering is that it includes leaven.
This indicates that the offerer still has sin and is therefore
in a weak condition.

III. FROM THE MEAL OFFERING THE OFFERER OFFERING ONE PIECE FROM EACH OFFERING AS A HEAVE OFFERING TO JEHOVAH, AND IT BEING FOR THE PRIEST WHO OFFERS THE PEACE OFFERING

"And from it he shall offer one from each offering as a
heave offering to Jehovah; it shall be for the priest who
dashes the blood of the peace offering" (v. 14). This has a
twofold significance. First, since the heave offering is a
type of Christ in His ascension, this signifies that Christ
as the meal offering in all His aspects is offered to God as
the One in ascension. Second, this signifies that such a
Christ is partaken of and enjoyed as food by the one who
ministers Christ as the peace offering. When we minister
the ascended Christ to others, we partake of the very
Christ whom we minister.

IV. THE FLESH OF THE THANKSGIVING SACRIFICE OF THE PEACE OFFERING BEING EATEN ON THE OFFERING DAY AND NO PART OF IT BEING LAID ASIDE UNTIL MORNING

"The flesh of the thanksgiving sacrifice of his peace

offering shall be eaten on the day it is offered; he shall not lay aside any of it until morning" (v. 15). This signifies that the maintaining power of this kind of offering is rather small, that it has to be fully enjoyed on the offering day, and that our experience and enjoyment of Christ in this aspect should be fresh daily.

We may be thankful to God and offer Him a peace offering. This is an offering in which we enjoy Christ in God's presence. However, the peace offering for thanksgiving is a weaker offering, and its enjoyment cannot be carried from one day to the next. The lasting power of this offering is not great.

V. THE SACRIFICE OF THE OFFERING, AS A VOW OR A FREEWILL OFFERING, BEING EATEN ON THE OFFERING DAY AND THE REMAINDER ON THE NEXT DAY

"But if the sacrifice of his offering is a vow or a freewill offering, it shall be eaten on the day he offers his sacrifice, and on the next day the remainder of it may be eaten" (v. 16). This signifies that the maintaining power of the peace offering for a vow or a freewill offering is stronger than that for thanksgiving, that it should be eaten on the offering day, and that our stronger enjoyment of Christ could last longer. If our offering is stronger, our enjoyment of this offering will last longer.

VI. THE FLESH OF THIS OFFERING EATEN ON THE THIRD DAY NOT BEING ACCEPTED BUT BEING AN ABHORRENT THING, AND THE EATER BEING CONDEMNED

"If any of the flesh of the sacrifice of his peace offering is eaten at all on the third day, it shall not be accepted; it shall not be accounted to him who offered it. It shall be an abhorrent thing, and the person who eats of it shall bear his iniquity" (v. 18). This signifies that our enjoyment of Christ in its oldness shall not be pleasant to God and not right with Him. The lawless enjoyment of Christ is abhorrent to God. Therefore, in 1 Corinthians 11 Paul warns us that in coming to the Lord's table, we must be careful.

VII. THE FLESH OF THIS OFFERING
TOUCHING ANYTHING UNCLEAN NOT BEING
EATEN BUT BURNED WITH FIRE

"The flesh that touches anything unclean shall not be eaten; it shall be burned with fire" (v. 19a). This signifies that the enjoyment of Christ as our peace should be kept from all uncleanness.

VIII. THE FLESH OF THE PEACE OFFERING
WHICH HAS NOT TOUCHED ANYTHING UNCLEAN BEING
EATEN BY THE PERSON WHO IS CLEAN

"And as for other flesh, anyone who is clean may eat of it" (v. 19b). This signifies that the enjoyment of Christ as our peace should not only be kept from all uncleanness but should also be eaten by a clean person.

IX. AN UNCLEAN PERSON WHO EATS THE FLESH
OF THE PEACE OFFERINGS THAT BELONG
TO JEHOVAH BEING CUT OFF FROM HIS PEOPLE

"But the person who eats the flesh of the sacrifice of peace offerings that belong to Jehovah while his uncleanness is upon him, that person shall be cut off from his people. And when a person touches anything unclean, whether the uncleanness of man, or an unclean beast, or any unclean abomination, and then eats of the flesh of the sacrifice of peace offerings that belong to Jehovah, that person shall be cut off from his people" (vv. 20-21). This signifies that the unclean person who partakes of Christ as his peace, as at the Lord's table (1 Cor. 10:16-17), shall be put aside from the fellowship of the enjoyment of Christ (cf. 1 Cor. 5:13b). An unclean person is a sinful person. Such a person should be removed from the fellowship at the Lord's table.

X. THE SONS OF ISRAEL NOT EATING
ANY FAT OF AN OX, A SHEEP, OR A GOAT

"You shall not eat any fat of an ox, a sheep, or a goat" (Lev. 7:23). This signifies that in their daily living the sons of Israel should consider God's food, as indicated by the fat of the ox, sheep, and goat, which fat signifies the tender, fine, and excellent part of the person of Christ.

This matter is crucial. As priests, in our eating we need to be concerned about God's food and should not eat the fat, which is God's portion. When we are practicing our priestly service, we are serving God, and we should consider not our own things but God's things. The fat, the top portion of the offerings, must not be eaten by the priests but must be offered to God for His satisfaction.

XI. THE FAT OF CATTLE
WHICH DIED OF THEMSELVES
OR WERE TORN BY BEASTS
NOT EATEN BY THE SONS OF ISRAEL
BUT PUT TO OTHER USES

"The fat of that which dies of itself and the fat of that which is torn by beasts may be put to any other use, but you shall certainly not eat it" (v. 24). This signifies that the dirtiness of death spoils the significance of God's enjoyment of Christ. God hates death and does not want to look upon anything related to it.

XII. WHOEVER EATS THE FAT
OF AN OFFERING BY FIRE OFFERED
TO JEHOVAH BEING CUT OFF FROM HIS PEOPLE

"Whoever eats the fat of a beast from which an offering by fire is offered to Jehovah, the person who eats shall be cut off from his people" (v. 25). This signifies that we who enjoy Christ as our offering to God should keep the excellent part of the person of Christ for God that we might not be put aside from the fellowship of the enjoyment of Christ. This fellowship of the enjoyment of Christ refers to the Lord's table. At the Lord's table, we have the fellowship of the enjoyment of Christ.

XIII. THE BLOOD, WHETHER OF BIRD OR
OF BEAST, NOT EATEN BY THE SONS OF ISRAEL

"Moreover, wherever you dwell you shall not eat any blood, whether of bird or of beast" (v. 26). This signifies that only the blood of Jesus should be taken by us for our redemption (John 6:53-56; Heb. 9:12).

XIV. ANY PERSON WHO EATS
ANY BLOOD BEING CUT OFF FROM HIS PEOPLE

"Any person who eats any blood, that person shall be cut off from his people" (v. 27). This signifies that anyone who regards the blood of Christ as a common thing shall be put aside from the fellowship of the enjoyment of Christ. We must regard the blood of Christ as special, particular, and precious. If we eat other blood, we make the blood of Christ common. This is sin.

XV. THE OFFERER OF THE PEACE OFFERING
BRINGING PARTS OF HIS OFFERING
FOR THE OFFERINGS OF JEHOVAH BY FIRE,
THE FAT BURNED TO GOD BY FIRE ON THE ALTAR
WITH THE BREAST AS A WAVE OFFERING
BEFORE JEHOVAH FOR AARON AND HIS SONS

"He who offers the sacrifice of his peace offerings to Jehovah shall bring his offering to Jehovah from the sacrifice of his peace offerings: his own hands shall bring the offerings of Jehovah by fire; he shall bring the fat with the breast, that the breast may be waved as a wave offering before Jehovah. And the priest shall offer up the fat in smoke on the altar; but the breast shall be for Aaron and his sons" (vv. 29-31). This signifies that we who take Christ as our peace offering should offer the excellent part of Christ (the fat) to God for His satisfaction, with the loving part of Christ (the breast) in resurrection for the serving ones' enjoyment.

The wave offering refers to Christ in His resurrection. The top part of the peace offering is for God; it is burned by fire and goes to God. The loving part, the breast, is allotted to us, the serving ones, for our enjoyment.

XVI. THE RIGHT THIGH OF THE PEACE OFFERING
GIVEN TO THE PRIEST AS A HEAVE OFFERING

"The right thigh you shall give to the priest as a heave offering from the sacrifices of your peace offerings. He from among Aaron's sons who offers the blood of the peace offerings and the fat, he shall have the right thigh for a portion" (vv. 32-33). This signifies that the part of strength of Christ (the right thigh) in His ascension is given to the serving one as a portion for his enjoyment.

Verses 29 through 33 reveal that the top part, the fat, goes to God and that the loving part, the breast, and also the part of strength, the right thigh, go to the serving ones. The more we minister Christ as the peace offering and the more we offer Christ as the peace offering to God, the more we will have the loving capacity and the strengthening power of Christ. In this way, we become stronger and more loving.

XVII. JEHOVAH HAVING TAKEN THE BREAST OF THE WAVE OFFERING AND THE THIGH OF THE HEAVE OFFERING OUT OF THE PEACE OFFERINGS AND HAVING GIVEN THEM TO THE PRIESTS AS THEIR PERPETUAL DUE

"I have taken the breast of the wave offering and the thigh of the heave offering from the sons of Israel out of the sacrifices of their peace offerings, and have given them to Aaron the priest and to his sons as their perpetual due from the sons of Israel" (v. 34). This signifies that God has allotted, in our enjoyment of Christ as the peace offering, the loving capacity and the strengthening power of Christ to us, the New Testament priests, as our eternal portion for our enjoyment in serving God.

XVIII. THIS BEING THE PORTION OF THE ANOINTING OF AARON AND HIS SONS FROM THE OFFERINGS OF JEHOVAH BY FIRE IN THE DAY WHEN THEY WERE BROUGHT TO SERVE JEHOVAH AS PRIESTS

"This is the portion of the anointing of Aaron and of the anointing of his sons from the offerings of Jehovah by fire, in the day when they were brought to serve Jehovah as priests. These Jehovah commanded to be given to them from the sons of Israel in the day when he anointed them; it is their perpetual due throughout their generations" (vv. 35-36). This signifies that the enjoyment of Christ's loving capacity and strengthening power is related to God's anointing of us for our priesthood.

We have been anointed by God to be priests, and God has allotted to us Christ's loving capacity and strengthening power. Hence, we can love and stand to serve God as priests.

XIX. THIS BEING THE LAW FOR THE BURNT OFFERING, THE MEAL OFFERING, THE SIN OFFERING, THE TRESPASS OFFERING, THE CONSECRATION, AND THE SACRIFICE OF PEACE OFFERINGS

"This is the law for the burnt offering, the meal offering, the sin offering, the trespass offering, the consecration offering, and the sacrifice of peace offerings, which Jehovah commanded Moses at Mount Sinai, in the day when He commanded the sons of Israel to offer their offerings to Jehovah, in the wilderness of Sinai" (vv. 37-38). This signifies that our consecration for the priesthood must be with the all-inclusive Christ as all the five offerings and according to their regulations.

Our text (v. 37) uses the term "the consecration offering." Actually, this should simply be "the consecration." There is not here a sixth offering called the consecration offering. Rather, the five offerings are for the consecration. At the time of consecration, God assigned these offerings, in different aspects, for the priests' enjoyment.

We have seen that in chapters one through five, the offerings are in a particular sequence: the burnt offering, the meal offering, the peace offering, the sin offering, and the trespass offering. This record is not according to doctrine but according to our practical experience. But in giving the laws of the five offerings, the sequence has changed greatly. Here the law of the burnt offering is first, followed by the law of the meal offering, of the sin offering, of the trespass offering, and of the peace offering. This latter sequence is according to the total picture of God's economy. In God's heart and in His desire, God would have Christ to be four kinds of offerings to us—the burnt offering, the meal offering, the sin offering, and the trespass offering. The burnt offering is the qualification for the sin offering, and the meal offering is the qualification for the trespass offering. With these four offerings, two are for the qualification, and two are for the result. The sin offering and the trespass offering are for a particular result. When these four offerings are in action, the result is peace. This peace is what God desires. God's heart is that we would enjoy His economy around His Son, Christ. Christ is our burnt offering, meal offering, sin offering, and trespass offering so that we may enjoy Him as peace. In our thanksgiving, in our vows, and in our freewill offerings, we enjoy Christ as our peace with God. This is the record of the totality of God's economy.

In Leviticus 1—7 we have two records: a record according to experience and a record according to God's economy in its totality. The four offerings—the burnt offering, the meal offering, the sin offering, and the trespass offering—are all for us to enjoy Christ as our peace with God in every way.

LIFE-STUDY OF LEVITICUS

THE CONSECRATION OF AARON AND HIS SONS

(1)

Scripture Reading: Lev. 8:1-21

In this message we will begin to consider the consecration of Aaron and his sons.

In Hebrew, the word *consecrate* (Exo. 28:41; 29:9, 33, 35) means "to fill the hands." Through Aaron's consecration to receive the holy position of high priest, his empty hands were filled (Lev. 8:25-28).

The word *consecration* is sometimes translated "ordination." Consecration is on our side; we consecrate ourselves to God. Ordination is on God's side; He ordains us.

As a result of my study of Exodus and Leviticus, I am convinced that for Aaron and his sons to be consecrated to serve as priests meant that their empty hands were filled. Aaron and his sons appeared empty-handed before Moses at the entrance of the tent of meeting. But when they were consecrated, their empty hands were filled with the type of Christ in different aspects.

The first seven chapters of Leviticus describe five categories of offerings: the burnt offering, the meal offering, the peace offering, the sin offering, and the trespass offering. Then five kinds of laws are given concerning the application of the five kinds of offerings. The result of the application of these offerings is peace. Peace is the totality of what Christ is to us with God. Under Christ's redemption, we are enjoying Christ as a totality, and this totality is peace, which implies rest, enjoyment, and satisfaction.

After the record of the offerings, Leviticus describes the

consecration of the priesthood. This indicates that the offerings in chapters one through seven are for the consecration, or ordination, of the priests.

According to the spiritual significance of this book, we all are priests. We have been reborn, regenerated, to be priests (Rev. 1:6; 5:10). As long as we have been regenerated, we are the real priests. However, we need a day of consecration on which we give ourselves to God and say, "Lord, I am Yours because You bought me. You redeemed me with Your blood, and You have regenerated me. Now that I have Your life and the enjoyment of Your redemption, I would like to offer myself to You. I give myself to You to serve You as Your servant, even as Your slave." God will immediately accept our offer and ordain us to be His serving ones, His priests. Thus, consecration is on our side, and ordination is on God's side.

Leviticus is not a book for ordinary people; it is a book for priests. Since we have been sanctified and separated from ordinary people, we are no longer common. We are a particular people—we are priests. All the offerings refer to Christ, and whatever Christ is to us and does for us is to constitute us priests. This constitution is the divine ordination.

God constitutes us to be something different from what we are by our natural birth. In our first birth, our original birth, we were constituted sinners (Rom. 5:19). Regardless of their class or social status, all human beings have been constituted sinners. All are sinners by birth. But through our second birth, we who believe in Christ have been constituted priests. Now we need our consecration and God's ordination to make our priesthood official.

Let us now consider the details concerning the consecration of Aaron and his sons.

I. AT THE ENTRANCE OF THE TENT OF MEETING

The consecration of Aaron and his sons took place at the entrance of the tent of meeting (Lev. 8:3-4). This signifies that our consecration for the priesthood is not only before God but also for the church life.

I like the expression "at the entrance of the tent of meeting." In Leviticus 8 the tent of meeting signifies the church life. We are God's priests in the church and for the church.

II. MOSES BRINGING AARON AND HIS SONS NEAR AND WASHING THEM WITH WATER

"Then Moses brought Aaron and his sons near and washed them with water" (v. 6). This signifies that for our consecration for the priesthood we need to be washed by the Spirit (1 Cor. 6:11).

Here Moses somewhat signifies Christ, and the water typifies the Holy Spirit. Christ washes us with the Holy Spirit. For the priesthood, which refers both to the priestly service and to a body of persons who are priests, we need to be washed by the Spirit. Therefore, 1 Corinthians 6:11 tells us that we have been washed, cleansed, by the Spirit.

III. MOSES CLOTHING AARON WITH THE HIGH PRIEST'S GARMENTS

In Leviticus 8:7-9 Moses clothed Aaron with the high priest's garments. "He put the tunic on him, girded him with the sash, clothed him with the robe, and put the ephod on him; and he girded him with the band of the ephod, and with it he bound it to him. And he put the breastplate on him, and in the breastplate he put the Urim and the Thummim. And he placed the turban upon his head, and on the turban, at its front, he placed the golden plate, the holy crown." This signifies that Christ as our High Priest is adorned with all the excellencies of His divine and human attributes and virtues. These attributes and virtues are Christ's garment. (See Life-study Messages on Exodus 28.)

IV. MOSES CLOTHING THE SONS OF AARON WITH THE PRIESTLY GARMENTS

"Then Moses brought Aaron's sons near and clothed them with tunics, girded them with sashes, and bound caps on them, as Jehovah had commanded Moses" (v. 13). Moses' clothing the sons of Aaron with priestly garments signifies that the New Testament priests are adorned with all the attributes and virtues of Christ.

The New Testament uses clothing to refer to our outward expression (Matt. 21:7; John 13:4). Our outward expression should be the expression of Christ's divine attributes. These attributes include the divine love, kindness, and holiness. Christ's divine attributes are expressed in human life as virtues. This means that the divine attributes become human virtues, and the human virtues are the expression of the divine attributes. The divine attributes and human virtues are not merely combined and united but mingled. For example, as a man Christ had human love, but this human love was mingled with the divine love. What God is (oil) was mingled with what Christ is (fine flour) in His humanity. In this way, God's nature was included in the expression of Christ's humanity. Because in Christ the divine attributes were mingled with the human virtues, His love, kindness, and mercy are extraordinary. In Him, the divine love, kindness, and mercy were mingled with the human love, kindness, and mercy.

This mingling of the divine attributes and the human virtues has become our clothing, because we who have been baptized into Christ have put on Christ (Gal. 3:27). To put on Christ is to be clothed with Christ. The very Christ with whom we are clothed is our priestly garment. Now whether we are a husband or a wife, a parent or a child, a teacher or a student, we should wear our priestly garment—a garment that is the expression of Christ's divine attributes mingled with His human virtues. Especially when we are going out to preach the gospel to sinners, we need to wear this garment. The expression of Christ should be our uniform. As we contact others, we need to impress them with the expression of Christ, that is, with the Christ with whom we are clothed. If we do this, we will have power and authority in our gospel preaching.

When we are ordained by God to serve Him as priests, He clothes us with Christ. One day you may consecrate yourself to the Lord to be a priest. Immediately, God,

Christ, and the Holy Spirit will adorn you. Sometimes the Lord's servants will work with the Triune God to adorn the saints with Christ. I am a little servant of God co-working with Him to adorn you with Christ, to help you to change your uniform from the uniform of your natural human life, culture, and nationality to the uniform of Christ. The different cultural uniforms divide, but the unique uniform of Christ makes us one.

V. MOSES ANOINTING THE TABERNACLE, THE ALTAR, AND THE LAVER WITH ALL THEIR UTENSILS TO SANCTIFY THEM

"Moses took the anointing oil and anointed the tabernacle and all that was in it, and sanctified them. And he sprinkled some of it on the altar seven times, and anointed the altar and all its utensils, and the laver and its base, to sanctify them" (Lev. 8:10-11). This signifies that Christ and the church, then the cross and the washing of the Spirit, are related to the New Testament priesthood for the priests' sanctification.

In the Bible, the tabernacle typifies Christ as an individual (John 1:14), and it also typifies the church as the dwelling place of God. In Leviticus 8 the tabernacle denotes the church much more than it denotes Christ. Moses anointed the priests, and he also anointed the tabernacle. The anointing of the tabernacle signifies the anointing of the church, in which we, the New Testament priests, serve God.

In ancient times, the priests and the tabernacle were two separate entities. Today the priests and the church are one and inseparable. We, the priests, are the church, and the church is we. Hence, for us today, the priests and the church are not two separate entities but one entity. Since we and the church are one, if we are anointed, the church also is anointed. Likewise, if the church is anointed, we also are anointed.

The altar in verse 11 refers to the burnt offering altar in the outer court. All the offerings were offered on this altar. The laver was a basin where the priests washed their hands and feet. The altar signifies the cross, and the laver signifies the Holy Spirit as the washing Spirit. In the washing Spirit is the washing water of life. The church, the cross, and the washing of the Spirit are all provisions for our practical consecration to be the priests today.

The church, the cross, and the washing Spirit are related to sanctification. Formerly, we were common; that is, we were not different from our relatives, neighbors, classmates, and colleagues. But now, having been consecrated and ordained to be God's priests, we are a sanctified people. To sanctify is to separate, to make particular, to make holy. We must be a group of people who are not only clean and pure but also separated, particular, and holy. We should be very different from the common people. This does not mean, however, that we need to wear peculiar clothing to show that we are sanctified. We should wear ordinary clothing, yet in this ordinary clothing there should be a consecration.

Regardless of our background, we all need to be sanctified, for we have consecrated ourselves to God, and He has ordained us. Do you not have the sense deep within that you have been ordained? One day, perhaps recently, you prayed, "Lord, I give myself to You absolutely." As long as you have prayed such a prayer, you have consecrated yourself to the Lord. God has accepted your consecration and has ordained you, filling your empty hands with Christ. God's ordination is signified by the word *sanctify*.

God's ordination is a matter of sanctification. Since God has sanctified us, we are no longer common.

The anointing brings the Triune God mingled with humanity to the priests and to the church life. This anointing includes Christ's human living, His death on the cross, and His resurrection. According to Exodus 30, the anointing oil is an ointment composed of oil, typifying the Spirit, compounded with four spices, signifying humanity (typified by the number four), human living, the death of the cross, and resurrection. When we are anointed as priests and as the church, we are anointed with the Triune

God compounded with Christ's humanity, human living, death, and resurrection. This anointing of the priests and the tabernacle also involves the sin offering (Lev. 8:14-17) and the burnt offering (vv. 18-21). All the elements of the anointing oil, the compound Spirit, with the sin offering and the burnt offering must be constituted into our being. Then we will be real priests to God, not by what we are through our natural birth but by the Triune God compounded with Christ's humanity, human living, death, resurrection, and ascension.

VI. MOSES ANOINTING AARON TO SANCTIFY HIM

Leviticus 8:12 tells us that Moses "poured some of the anointing oil upon Aaron's head, and anointed him to sanctify him." This signifies that Christ as our High Priest was anointed by God for His sanctification.

VII. A BULL AS THE SIN OFFERING FOR THE CONSECRATION OF THE PRIESTHOOD

Verses 14 through 17 speak of the bull of the sin offering for the consecration of the priesthood. This offering signifies the stronger and richer Christ as our sin offering for the assuming of our New Testament priesthood. (For details, see Life-study Messages on Exodus 29.)

The sin offering deals with our natural man, our flesh, the personified sin that dwells in us, Satan, the world hanging on Satan, and the power struggle. If we would be New Testament priests, all these things must be dealt with by Christ as the sin offering. When Christ was crucified as our sin offering, He dealt with the natural man, the flesh, the indwelling sin, Satan, the world, and the power struggle. In the divine ordination, such a sin offering is applied to us that we may be prevailing priests serving God.

VIII. A RAM AS THE BURNT OFFERING FOR THE CONSECRATION OF THE PRIESTHOOD

Verses 18 through 21 speak of the ram of the burnt offering for the consecration of the priesthood. This burnt offering, which is also included in God's ordination of the priests, signifies the strong Christ as our burnt offering for the assuming of our New Testament priesthood. The burnt offering reminds us that as serving ones we must be absolute for God. Because we are not absolute for God, we need to take Christ as our burnt offering.

LIFE-STUDY OF LEVITICUS

PART ONE — MESSAGE TWENTY-NINE

THE CONSECRATION OF AARON AND HIS SONS

(2)

Scripture Reading: Lev. 8:14-29

In this message we will consider further the consecration of Aaron and his sons.

In the consecration of the priesthood, the first thing carried out was the anointing of the priests. This indicates strongly that the consecration or anointing of the priesthood is to make God one with us, for the anointing oil signifies that whatever God is, whatever He does, and whatever He will do are ours. What God has done, what He is doing, and what He will do involve many things, such as Christ's incarnation, human living, death, resurrection, ascension, and coming back. All this has been anointed upon us, that is, made one with us. This is the positive side of the ordination of the priesthood.

In the consecration of Aaron and his sons, the offerings immediately followed the anointing. The offerings remind us of who and what we are, and of what we should be yet are not.

The sin offering is the first to do such a reminding. Aaron had been anointed with the anointing oil, which signifies that the Triune God with all that He is, has done, and will do was now Aaron's. This anointing also indicates that Aaron was one with the Triune God. However, this anointed one still needed a strong reminding that by himself and in himself he was sin, a sin-constituted sinner, and flesh with nothing good in him; that he was a natural man, a part of the old creation, which is absolutely saturated, possessed, usurped, and indwelt by the evil one; and that he was filled with the world and the power struggle.

The Triune God had ordained Aaron to be His serving one and had anointed him with Himself. However, Aaron still needed to realize what he was. Thus, God used the sin offering to remind him of what he was. On the first day of Aaron's priesthood and every day thereafter, he had to offer the sin offering to God so that he would be reminded of what he was.

We today are God's priests. He has chosen, appointed, and ordained us to be His holy priests. Whatever the Triune God has done, is doing, and will do is ours. He is one with us, and we are one with Him. However, we still need to be reminded that, in ourselves, we are sin, flesh, and the old man, that we are the old creation, which is saturated with Satan, the evil one, and that we are filled with the world and its power struggle. If every day and all during the day the brothers, co-workers, and elders would remember this, being reminded of what they are, the situation among us would be different.

Concerning our life and work, we need to ask ourselves whether the one moving, acting, and doing things is the old man or God's priest. Do you have the assurance to say that whatever you are doing in the church life, in the Lord's work, and in the recovery is of the divine priesthood and not of the flesh? Who can say that his hands are clean and that he is absolutely free from the flesh? Because we cannot say this, we need the sin offering as it is typified in Leviticus. We need this offering not only to be forgiven by God but also to be reminded of what we are. Even in loving others we need to be reminded that we are sin, flesh, the old man, and the old creation and that we are filled with worldliness. If we love others according to our flesh, taste, and choice, our love is sinful in the eyes of God, for such a love is linked to the evil one. Furthermore, as we pray and share in the meetings, we may have thoughts that come from the flesh, where sin is hidden and where Satan moves secretly. This is our actual situation. Thus, we need the sin offering not only at the time of our ordination as priests but also every time we practice our priesthood.

In the ordination of the priests a ram was used for a burnt offering. The burnt offering reminds us that we should be absolute for God yet we are not. As ordained priests of God, we should therefore receive His mercy and grace to be absolute for God in Christ, with Christ, and through Christ.

Since Aaron had been anointed by God, why did he still need the burnt offering? Aaron needed this offering because God wanted Aaron to be reminded that he should be absolute for God yet he was not. This should remind us that we today are likewise not absolute for God. It should also warn us that every day we need to offer a burnt offering. Daily we need to offer a burnt offering for our priesthood, for our priestly service. The elders and co-workers in particular should offer the burnt offering every morning. We should tell the Lord, "Lord, throughout this day remind me that I should be absolute for You. Yet, I realize that I am not and cannot be absolute for You. Lord, I trust in You and take You as my life, my person, and my absoluteness. My absoluteness for God is You, Lord." This is to live Christ.

We may be familiar with the words "live Christ," but we may not understand the real significance of living Christ. Do we live Christ at home and in the church life? In our family life and in our dealing with the saints, are we absolute for God? When our self-feeling or self-interest is touched by others, we may become offended. Does this not indicate that we are not absolute for God? We surely need to be reminded that, in ourselves, we are not absolute for God.

According to Leviticus, the burnt offering should be offered every morning (6:12-13). The burning of the burnt offering should not cease. "The burnt offering itself shall be upon the hearth on the altar all night until the morning, and the fire of the altar shall be kept burning on it" (6:9). This indicates that the burnt offering should burn through the dark night of this age until morning, until the Lord Jesus comes again.

IX. THE SECOND RAM AS THE CONSECRATION OFFERING FOR THE CONSECRATION OF THE PRIESTHOOD

The second ram was used as a consecration offering (7:37) for the consecration of the priesthood (8:22-32). This ram signifies the strong Christ for our assuming of the New Testament priesthood. We need a strong Christ for our consecration.

A. Some of the Blood Put on Aaron's and His Sons' Right Ear, Thumb of Their Right Hand, and Big Toe of Their Right Foot

"Moses took some of its blood and put it on the tip of Aaron's right ear, and on the thumb of his right hand, and on the big toe of his right foot. And he brought Aaron's sons near, and Moses put some of the blood on the tip of their right ear, and on the thumb of their right hand, and on the big toe of their right foot" (8:23-24a). This signifies that the redeeming blood of Christ cleanses our ears, our hands, and our feet for the assuming of our New Testament priesthood. The service of the New Testament priesthood includes functioning in the meetings, preaching the gospel, and visiting the saints in their homes. For all these services, we need the cleansing of the blood of Christ.

Our moving (feet) and working (hands) are always under the direction of our hearing. We act according to what we hear. Therefore, in the church life, hearing is crucial.

By hearing we have been saved, and by hearing we may be nourished and edified. However, by hearing we may also be damaged and killed, and we may do evil things to others because of what we hear. Our hearing is a problem. In 2 Timothy 4:3 Paul speaks of those who "heap up to themselves teachers tickling the ear." Therefore, God's dealing must first touch the source—our hearing.

If any church would stop hearing negative things, that church would be very healthy and living. The church that is the weakest and the most deadened is the one full of criticism, gossip, and reasoning.

The principle is the same in married life. A certain brother may be very living. But if his wife speaks to him in a negative way, he will be poisoned and deadened and will find it hard to pray in the church meeting. Likewise, if a brother passes on a negative word to his wife, she will be deadened by it. These illustrations from the church life and from married life show the importance of hearing.

Since we are God's priests, we need to ask ourselves what kind of things we are willing to hear. Do we intend to hear positive things or negative things? Because we often hear unclean things, things that are unhealthy and contagious, we need to wash our ears with the blood of Christ. According to the Bible, where the blood washes, there the Spirit anoints. After the washing of the blood, we will enjoy the anointing of the Spirit. Then we will forget the negative things we heard, or at least we will not repeat these things. We will also become healthy and living, and the church will go on in our health.

Wherever we go, we need to take care of our hearing. If we do this, whatever we hear will be right and positive. Then we will go the right way and do the right work. However, if we do not take care of our hearing but give ear to negative speaking, our deeds and work will be affected in a negative way.

The purpose of the consecration offering (Lev. 8:23) is not to deal with our sin and trespasses but to deal particularly with our ear, our thumb, and our toe, that is, with our listening, our working, and our acting. If we are not careful about our ears, we will be gossipers and those who spread reasonings and debates. Then instead of ministering Christ, we will spread death. Today some devote themselves to spreading death and not to spreading Christ, the truth, and the gospel. Our listening ear, our working hand, and our walking toe must be redeemed by the blood of Christ. We must let the blood of Christ release us from all the negative things. Then all the positive things of Christ will fill our hands.

B. Moses Dashing the Blood on the Altar All Around

Leviticus 8:24b says, "Then Moses dashed the blood on

the altar all around." This signifies that the blood of the redeeming Christ is for the redemption from our sin.

C. One Unleavened Cake, One Cake of Oiled Bread, and One Wafer Placed upon the Portions of the Fat and upon the Right Thigh, All These Put on the Palms of Aaron and of His Sons, Waved as a Wave Offering before Jehovah, Taken from Their Palms and Offered Up in Smoke upon the Altar upon the Burnt Offering for a Consecration Offering by Fire to Jehovah for a Satisfying Fragrance

In 8:25-28 we see that one unleavened cake, one cake of oiled bread, and one wafer were placed upon the portions of the fat and upon the right thigh. Then all these portions were put on the palms of Aaron and of his sons, waved as a wave offering, taken from their hands, and offered up in smoke upon the altar upon the burnt offering for a consecration offering by fire to Jehovah for a satisfying fragrance. This signifies that the tender, excellent, and strong parts of Christ, with the three kinds of cakes, with His sinless but Spirit-mingled humanity in different aspects as food, are offered to God in Christ's resurrection as a satisfying and fragrant offering in the fellowship of His sufferings unto death on the cross for our assuming of the New Testament priesthood.

Leviticus 8:26 speaks of "one unleavened cake, and one cake of oiled bread, and one wafer." This verse also refers to the fat and the right thigh. The unleavened cake, the cake of oiled bread, and the one wafer indicate respectively that we have Christ as our daily food without sin, that we have Christ as our daily food mingled with the Spirit, and that we have Christ as the food that is so available and easy to take in and that is good for feeding the young ones. We feed ourselves with the cakes, and we feed others with the wafers. The fat signifies the portion of Christ that is for God, and the right thigh signifies Christ as our strength to stand.

Verse 27 says, "Then he put all these on the palms of Aaron and on the palms of his sons, and waved them as a wave offering before Jehovah." Through this filling of the hands, they became consecrated, ordained priests. Today our hands can also be filled with the all-inclusive Christ, with the Christ who is the unleavened cake, the cake mingled with oil, the wafer, the fat, and the right thigh. We have the Christ who is God's portion (the fat) and the Christ who is our standing power (the right thigh). We also have Christ as cakes to feed ourselves and as wafers to feed others, especially the young ones.

All these things were waved before Jehovah. This means that they were a wave offering, which signifies Christ in resurrection. Nothing here is natural; rather, everything is in Christ's resurrection. In resurrection Christ is food for us and for the young ones. In resurrection Christ is also God's portion and our standing power.

"Moses took them from their palms and offered them up in smoke on the altar upon the burnt offering; they were a consecration offering for a satisfying fragrance, an offering by fire to Jehovah" (v. 28). Here we see that the consecration offering is not merely a ram but has been increased to include other items. This all-inclusive offering was offered in Christ's resurrection to God for His satisfaction.

If we intend to be New Testament priests, we need to take care of all the matters signified in these verses. In order to function as New Testament priests, preaching the gospel, functioning in the church, visiting people in their homes, and caring for the saints, we need to pay attention to all that is covered in 8:24-28. In particular, we need to realize that the priesthood is a burning service. In this service we burn ourselves and cause others to be burned. This burning is upon Christ's burning. As we burn upon Christ's burning, we have the fellowship of Christ's sufferings unto death on the cross for the practice of the New Testament priesthood.

D. The Breast Waved as a Wave
Offering before Jehovah for Moses' Portion

"Moses took the breast and waved it as a wave offering

before Jehovah; it was Moses' portion from the ram of consecration, as Jehovah had commanded Moses" (v. 29). This signifies that the loving capacity of Christ in His resurrection is for the one who ministers Christ to us in our consecration for the priesthood.

This verse indicates that the serving one deserves a particular portion of Christ. When you preach Christ, you deserve Christ. When you preach the gospel, you deserve the rich enjoyment of the gospel. Whenever we, the serving ones, minister Christ to others, we deserve to enjoy the very Christ we minister to them.

LIFE-STUDY OF LEVITICUS

PART ONE — MESSAGE THIRTY

THE CONSECRATION OF AARON AND HIS SONS

(3)

Scripture Reading: Lev. 8:30-36

Before we consider some further matters related to the consecration of Aaron and his sons, I would like to give an additional word concerning the application of the blood to the right ear, the right thumb, and the big toe of the right foot and also a word about putting the offering on the palms of the priests.

Some of the blood of the ram of consecration was put on Aaron's and his sons' right ear, on the thumb of their right hand, and on the big toe of their right foot. This signifies that the redeeming blood of Christ cleanses our ears for hearing, our hands for working, and our feet for walking. This is for the assuming of our New Testament priesthood.

Our hearing is mentioned first because it affects our working and our moving. The blood of Christ deals with our ear for listening to God's word, to God's speaking. To serve God as priests, we should be faithful slaves, or servants, to God. As Isaiah 50:4 and 5 indicate, a servant must have a hearing ear. A servant who does not listen to his master's word cannot serve him according to his will, heart, and desire.

When we were sinners, we did not have an ear to listen to God's word, to God's speaking. Daily we listened to many other things, but we did not listen to the word of God. Now that we have been saved and ordained as God's priests, His servants, the primary thing is to listen to God's speaking. In typology, when a slave wanted to stay with his master, the master brought him to the doorpost and pierced his ear (Exo. 21:2-6), indicating that the slave must be keen to listen to the master's word. As God's priests today, we must learn to listen to His word.

The first thing that we as God's priests need to deal with is our listening. Positive listening will rescue us from negative listening. If we listen to God's word from morning to evening, we will not have an ear to listen to any negative speaking. Negative talk prevails and spreads in the church life because certain ones turn their ears from God to something else. These ones do not speak Christ, the word of God, grace, or the gospel. Instead, they listen to negative things, and they work and move according to the negative things they hear. The result is the spreading of death. If we turn our ears from other things back to God Himself, there will not be any problems, and only life will be spreading, not death.

The principle is the same in our married life. If a sister wants to have a good husband, she should not speak to him negatively but should talk to him about God, Christ, grace, the gospel, and the divine light. This kind of speaking will build up her husband and cause him to seek the Lord. However, if she speaks negatively to her husband, she will deaden him. The same is true, both positively and negatively, of the way a brother speaks to his wife. We all need to be careful about our listening. We need to have the redeeming blood of Christ applied to our ear, our thumb, and our toe.

The cleansing of the right ear, the right thumb, and the big toe of the right foot was needed on two occasions: at the ordination of the priests and at the time of the cleansing of a leper (Lev. 14:14). Both the lepers and the priests needed to have their ear, thumb, and toe cleansed with the redeeming blood. This indicates that in the eyes of God we sinners who have been ordained as God's priests are lepers. As God's priests, His servants, we need to have our ears redeemed from listening to anything other than God and have them brought back to listening to the word of God. Also, we need to have our working hand redeemed from doing anything other than God's work. Furthermore, our toe for walking also needs to be redeemed.

In 8:26-28 we see that one unleavened cake, one cake of oiled bread, and one wafer (belonging to the meal offering) were placed upon the portions of the fat and the right thigh (another category of offerings). These two categories of offerings as a whole were put on the palms of Aaron and his sons. At that point, the hands of Aaron and of his sons were no longer empty. These offerings were then waved before Jehovah (v. 27), probably by those whose hands had been filled with them. This waving signifies Christ's move in His resurrection. The offerings were first "killed," and then they were waved, that is, resurrected, thereby becoming offerings before Jehovah in Christ's resurrection.

The two cakes, the wafer, the fat, and the thigh were then offered up in smoke (indicating a slow burning to bring out the flavor) upon the burnt offering for a consecration offering by fire to Jehovah for a satisfying fragrance (v. 28). This satisfying fragrance is for God alone; it is His portion for His enjoyment. The tender, excellent parts (the fat), the strong part (the right thigh), and the two cakes and the one wafer—signifying different aspects of Christ's sinless and Spirit-mingled humanity—are food not for the priests but for God. God's portion was offered on the altar, which signifies the cross. This indicates that we offer God's food in the fellowship of Christ's suffering unto the death of the cross. Although this is for God's satisfaction, it is also for our assuming of the New Testament priesthood.

We may proclaim the fact that we are God's priests, but probably none among us ever realized how many matters are involved in being a priest. Fifty-five years ago I did not know that I needed the sin offering to remind me that I am nothing but flesh, an old man in the old creation who is linked with Satan, the world, and the struggle for power. I claimed to be a priest of God, yet I practiced my priesthood in ignorance. I did not know that to be a priest in the New Testament priesthood I needed Christ's humanity, His strengthening power, and His loving capacity (signified by the breast waved as a wave offering—v. 29). If we all check our past, God's light of grace will expose where we were as

God's priests—in the old creation, in the flesh, and in the natural life with the natural love, the natural affection. Concerning this, we all need to be exposed and cleansed. We need the cleansing blood on the tip of our right ear, on our right thumb, and on the big toe of our right foot.

E. Moses Sprinkling Aaron and His Sons and Their Garments with the Anointing Oil and Some of the Blood to Sanctify Them

"Moses took some of the anointing oil and some of the blood which was on the altar, and sprinkled it on Aaron, on his garments, on his sons and on the garments of his sons with him; and he sanctified Aaron, his garments, and his sons and the garments of his sons with him" (v. 30). This signifies that God sprinkles us, the New Testament priests, and our conduct (garments), with the compounded Spirit and the redeeming blood of the cross of Christ to separate us, to make us holy unto Him.

No matter how much God has been working on us, dealing with our sin, our natural life, and the old man, we still need more "coats" of the anointing oil. The anointing oil refers to the processed Triune God with all that He has become, has done, and has passed through. Such a Triune God, who has been processed and has been compounded with the "spices" of incarnation, human living, an all-inclusive death, a wonderful resurrection, and an excellent ascension, has become the anointing oil, the ointment, to "paint" us (Exo. 30:23-30). We need to be painted again and again with the processed Triune God as the anointing oil.

In order to have the proper knowledge of our New Testament priesthood, we need to study the book of Leviticus. Leviticus is not only for the Old Testament saints. If we understand the typology of this book, we will see that point after point applies to us in a practical way today.

F. The Flesh with the Bread of the Consecration Offering Eaten by the Priests at the Entrance of the Tent of Meeting

"Then Moses said to Aaron and to his sons, Boil the

flesh at the entrance of the tent of meeting, and eat it there with the bread which is in the basket of the consecration offering, as I have commanded, saying, Aaron and his sons shall eat it" (v. 31). This signifies that Christ as the redeeming One with His humanity is food to us (John 6:51), the New Testament priests, at the entering in of the church life.

In Leviticus 8:28 we have God's portion, and in verse 31 we have our portion. The flesh here refers to Christ as the redeeming One, and the bread refers to His humanity. Christ as the redeeming One with His humanity is our food.

G. The Remains of the Flesh
and of the Bread Burned with Fire

"What remains of the flesh and of the bread you shall burn with fire" (v. 32). This signifies that the inexhaustible riches of Christ should be kept by God's holiness.

Verse 32 indicates that the Christ whom we offer to God for His enjoyment and whom we also enjoy is inexhaustible. After God's portion has been offered to Him and we have enjoyed our portion, something still remains. In Leviticus 8 the remainder was burned with fire, which signifies God's holiness. From this we see that the inexhaustible riches of Christ should be kept in and by God's holiness.

X. THE CONSECRATING PRIESTS REMAINING AT THE ENTRANCE OF THE TENT OF MEETING FOR SEVEN DAYS FOR THEIR PROPITIATION

The consecrating priests remained at the entrance of the tent of meeting for seven days for their propitiation (8:33-36). This signifies that our assuming of the New Testament priesthood should be thorough and complete for our propitiation at the entering in of the church life.

Verses 33 through 35 say, "You shall not go out from the entrance of the tent of meeting for seven days, until the day when the period of your consecration is fulfilled; for you shall be consecrated seven days. As it was done this

day, so Jehovah has commanded to do, to make propitiation for you. You shall remain at the entrance of the tent of
meeting day and night for seven days, and keep the charge
of Jehovah, that you may not die; for so I have been
commanded." The same procedure was repeated for seven
days. Each day the program was carried out in a solemn
way, for every aspect of the program was solemn. This
solemnity is indicated by the words "that you may not
die." Therefore, no one dared to be careless or loose.
Everyone was aware of the seriousness of what was taking
place and of what might happen if anyone was careless.

These verses should be a warning to us not to enter into
the enjoyment of Christ in a careless way. We especially
need this warning with respect to the Lord's table. The
bread signifies Christ's body, and the wine signifies His
blood. If we eat the bread and drink the wine without the
proper discernment, our eating and drinking could be to
our own judgment (1 Cor. 11:27-29). We need to be warned
of the seriousness of participating in the fellowship in the
enjoyment of Christ in a light or loose way.

The consecration of the priesthood lasted for seven
days, with the same things repeated each day. Through
this repetition, Aaron and his sons were no doubt deeply
impressed with every matter. As God's priests today, we
also need to remember all the things involved in our
consecration and ordination as priests. In particular, we
need to be reminded that, in ourselves, we are sinners, even
the flesh of sin.

The consecration of Aaron and his sons is solemn not
only in its typology but also in its application to us today.
If we realize the seriousness of this matter, we will also
realize how much we need the Lord's mercy and the
cleansing of His blood. We will ask the Lord to be merciful
to us, and we will hide under the covering of His blood.

LIFE-STUDY OF LEVITICUS

PART ONE — MESSAGE THIRTY-ONE

THE INITIATION OF THE PRIESTLY SERVICE OF AARON AND HIS SONS

Scripture Reading: Lev. 9:1-21

The book of Leviticus shows us a new beginning, in which, for the first time, God's people offered offerings to God according to God's regulations. This was the first time God's people offered Christ to God not merely according to their need but also according to God's laws, His regulations. Before that time, some, such as Abel, Noah, and Abraham, offered to God, but it was not until the Israelites kept the Passover (Exo. 12:1-28) that offerings were presented to God according to His instructions. Strictly speaking, although the Passover lamb was an offering, it was not called an offering.

In Leviticus, after the erecting of the tabernacle, God had a dwelling place on earth from within which He spoke to His people. The first category of speaking concerned the offerings (Lev. 1—7). The offerings were not only needed by man and requested by God but were also ordained by God in regulations which were absolutely according to God's mind and desire. Moses should have realized the significance of these offerings in regard to the matter of propitiation (Lev. 9:7), yet in the details of the offerings he may have understood very little.

In Leviticus the Israelites began to practice offering to God in a way which had never been done before. The offerings were now offered to God not by an individual but by a people, a congregation, and not at the place of their choice. God asked the people to come to the entrance of the tent of meeting to contact Him and to offer their offerings by priests, not by themselves. (This is different from the offering of the offerings by Abel, Noah, and

Abraham, who were not only offerers but serving priests.) The manner in which the offerings were offered became a ceremony, a form, to be carried out before God at the entrance of His dwelling place according to His regulations, laws, and arrangement. All this was surely something new.

Although Moses did not see that the offerings were Christ, God was actually giving commands to His people about how to apply Christ as all the offerings according to God's laws. We today need to learn how to apply Christ according to God's requests. Early in the morning, we need to apply Christ as our burnt offering, sin offering, and meal offering so that we may have something to live by during the day.

Let us now consider the record in Leviticus 9:1-21 regarding the initiation of the priestly service of Aaron and his sons.

I. ON THE EIGHTH DAY

The initiation of the priestly service of Aaron and his sons took place on the eighth day (v. 1), which signifies resurrection (Mark 16:9a). This indicates that all the priestly service must be in resurrection (cf. Rev. 20:6).

The eighth day in Leviticus 9:1 refers to the day after the seven days of the consecration of Aaron and his sons. During each of these seven days, Aaron and his sons went through the same procedure. On the eighth day, the day after that course of consecration, they had a new beginning. The eighth day thus implies both a new beginning and the ending of the oldness.

As priests of God, our priesthood, our priestly service, must be altogether in resurrection. The natural life, the old man, and the flesh have no ground here. Unfortunately, however, in our actual church life there are many natural things, and there is much oldness. Such things are not on the eighth day; that is, they are not in the realm of resurrection but in the realm of the natural life.

We condemn evil things, but we may not condemn those

good things which are done in the old creation. For example, we condemn hatred, but we may not condemn a love
which is natural and not in the Spirit. In the New Testament, on the contrary, there is a concern regarding natural
love, which is actually a kind of "honey." According
to Leviticus 2, neither leaven nor honey was allowed to
be added to the meal offering. Leaven refers to what is
evil, and honey, to what is naturally good. Whereas natural
hatred is leaven, natural love is honey. Natural hatred
is evil, but natural love is good. However, both good and
evil are from the same source—the tree of the knowledge
of good and evil. Since natural hatred and natural love
are natural, both belong to the tree of the knowledge
of good and evil; and since both belong to this tree, both
should be condemned. This is the reason that when, in the
Gospel of John, the Lord Jesus was asked questions
regarding good and evil, right and wrong, yes and no, He
referred the people to life. The Lord's concern is life, not
good and evil.

The priestly service we render to God must be in
resurrection. The reality of resurrection is Christ as the
life-giving Spirit (1 Cor. 15:45b). Anything we do in the
Spirit is on the eighth day, in resurrection. Anything we do
outside the Spirit, in our natural life, mind, or emotion, is
not on the eighth day, not in resurrection.

I hope that all the saints, including the newly saved
ones, will receive this word concerning the priestly service
on the eighth day. When you intend to show love toward a
particular person, you need to consider whether this love
arises from your spirit or from your natural emotion. Is
this love a matter of your natural likes or dislikes, a matter
of liking one person but not another? Further, because of
your natural love for a certain one, you may treat that one
in a preferential way. This is honey, and honey eventually
ferments and becomes the same as leaven. This means
that, in the eyes of God, natural love is just as evil as
natural hatred.

Quite often the Lord will require us to love someone
whom we cannot love in our natural life and with our

natural love. The only way we can love that one is with a love which is not natural but is in resurrection. All our service must be in spirit, in resurrection.

II. AARON PREPARING HIS
SIN OFFERING AND HIS BURNT OFFERING
AND MAKING PROPITIATION
FOR HIMSELF AND FOR THE PEOPLE

Leviticus 9:7 says, "Then Moses said to Aaron, Come near to the altar and prepare your sin offering and your burnt offering, and make propitiation for yourself and for the people; and prepare the offering of the people, and make propitiation for them, as Jehovah has commanded." In this verse we see that Aaron was to make propitiation for himself and for the people. The term *propitiation* needs to be distinguished from the terms *redemption* and *atonement*, for these words do not have the same meaning; there are important differences. Redemption was completed by the Lord Jesus' death on the cross and this term should be used only for the New Testament. Before He shed His blood on the cross, there was not such a thing as redemption. What we have in the Old Testament is propitiation. Sometimes the Hebrew word for propitiation is translated "atonement." Atonement is a matter of at-one-ment; it refers to appeasing the situation between two parties in order to bring them together, to make them one. Propitiation refers to the appeasing of a situation between two parties by doing something for one party to satisfy the demands of the other party.

As sinners, we had a problem with our righteous God. Although He loved us, something unrighteous existed between us and Him. Not until this unrighteous situation was appeased could we be one with God. Therefore, on the cross Christ accomplished redemption for us. Christ not only shed His blood to accomplish redemption, but in His ascension He entered into the heavens and presented His blood before God. Through this presentation of His blood, He acquired, gained, an eternal redemption for us (Heb. 9:12). When we believed into Christ, we entered into Him and received this redemption.

How did God deal with the sins of the Old Testament saints before Christ came? God covered their sins, but He did not remove them. Paul tells us clearly that "it is impossible for the blood of bulls and goats to take away sins" (Heb. 10:4). Rather, with such sacrifices there was "a calling to mind of sins year by year" (v. 3) at the feast of propitiation. The sins of the Old Testament saints remained, but these sins were covered. This covering took place on the propitiation cover (Rom. 3:25), which was the lid of the ark of the testimony. Inside the ark were the two tablets, with five of the Ten Commandments inscribed on each. The Ten Commandments condemned anyone who approached God. But the blood of the sin offering shed on the day of propitiation was sprinkled on the lid of the ark for the making of propitiation. Hence, the cover of the ark was known as the propitiation cover.

In Leviticus 9:7 Aaron was told to make propitiation for himself and for the people. He had a problem with God, and he needed to do something to appease the situation so that he could have peace with God.

A. Signifying That Aaron as a Sinful Person Needed to Take Christ as His Sin Offering and Burnt Offering for Him to Be a Priest to Serve God

Aaron's preparing his sin offering and burnt offering and making propitiation for himself first signifies that he, as a sinful person, needed to take Christ as his sin offering and burnt offering for him to be a priest to serve God. Before he could serve as a priest, Aaron had to have his situation appeased. He needed the sin offering and also the burnt offering.

Today the sin offering reminds us of many negative things, and the burnt offering reminds us that we should be absolute for God, yet we are not. We need to take Christ as our sin offering to redeem us back to a peaceful situation with God, and we need to take Christ as the burnt offering, as the One who lives in us and for us a life that is absolutely for God.

B. Signifying That Aaron Typified Christ Offering Himself as a Sin Offering for the Redemption of God's People and as a Burnt Offering for God's People to Be God's Satisfaction

Aaron's preparing the sin offering and the burnt offering also signifies that Aaron typifies Christ's offering Himself as a sin offering for the redemption of God's people and as a burnt offering for God's people to be God's satisfaction. In the sin offering God's people are one with Christ; hence, we are redeemed in Him. He has acquired, gained, redemption. As long as we are one with Him, we have redemption. In the burnt offering Christ is one with God's people; hence, He is living in us that we may live Him for God's satisfaction.

The sin offering is something in death, and the burnt offering is something in resurrection. We are one with Christ in His death, and He is one with us in His resurrection.

C. Signifying That Whatever Christ as Our High Priest Did, He Did for Us, That We Might Be Redeemed from Sin and Made God's Satisfaction

Finally, Aaron's preparing the sin offering and the burnt offering signifies that whatever Christ as our High Priest did, He did for us, that we might be redeemed from sin and made God's satisfaction. In the living Christ we are made God's satisfaction by living absolutely for Him.

III. AARON OFFERING FOR THE PEOPLE THE SIN OFFERING, THE BURNT OFFERING, AND THE MEAL OFFERING

"Then he brought the offering of the people, and took the goat of the sin offering which was for the people and slaughtered it, and he offered it for sin, like the first. And he brought the burnt offering, and offered it according to the ordinance. He also brought the meal offering and filled his palms with it, and offered it up in smoke on the altar in addition to the burnt offering of the morning" (vv. 15-17). This signifies that Christ offered Himself for us as our sin offering to deal with our sin, as our burnt offering to satisfy God, and as our meal offering to be God's food and also our food. Every morning we should take Christ as these offerings, praying, "Lord, for this new day I take You as my sin offering, burnt offering, and meal offering, that I may live by You, with You, and in You and even live You for God's satisfaction."

IV. AARON OFFERING FOR THE PEOPLE
THE PEACE OFFERING

In 9:18-21 we see that Aaron offered the peace offering for the people. This signifies that Christ offered Himself as our peace offering for us and God to enjoy Him as peace. We enjoy this peace as we enjoy Christ at the Lord's table.

The enjoyment of Christ as the peace offering in verses 18 through 21 is based upon Christ as our sin offering, burnt offering, and meal offering, as covered in verses 7 through 17. Perhaps you are wondering why there is no mention of the trespass offering in these verses. Here the trespass offering is included in the sin offering.

This is the first time in human history that Christ is applied in such a way and to such an extent. In this application Christ is our sin offering, our burnt offering, and then our meal offering for our daily living, with the result that we enter into peace, which is Christ Himself. This is the initiation of the offerings, pointing to the living Christ, whom we are enjoying and eating every day as our daily food.

LIFE-STUDY OF LEVITICUS

PART ONE — MESSAGE THIRTY-TWO

THE ISSUE OF THE PRIESTLY SERVICE

Scripture Reading: Lev. 9:4, 6, 22-24

In this message we will pay our attention to the issue, the result, of our priestly service. It is difficult to speak about the result of our priesthood because this issue is not something material but something spiritual, mysterious, heavenly, and divine. The issue of the New Testament priestly service is the appearing of God to us (v. 4), the appearing of God's glory to us (vv. 6, 23b), the divine blessing (vv. 22-23), and the consuming fire (v. 24). Let us now consider each of these matters.

I. THE APPEARING OF GOD TO US

The appearing of God to us is related to our taking Christ as the offerings. As we confess our mistakes, failures, and wrongdoings, we spontaneously take Christ as our sin offering and trespass offering. This may lead us to take Him as our burnt offering. We may tell Him, "Lord Jesus, You are my burnt offering. I cannot be absolute for God, but You can. Now I take You, Lord, as my absoluteness for God." This kind of prayer indicates that we desire to live Christ for God's satisfaction. The sin offering and the burnt offering will then lead us to take Christ as the meal offering. We will offer the top portion to God as His food, and we will feed on Christ as our daily food, as our daily life supply. Furthermore, we will be brought into a sense of peace, into a tranquil situation, and enjoy Christ as our peace, rest, satisfaction, and comfort. As the issue of taking Christ as all these offerings, God's presence will be with us. This is the appearing of God to us. We cannot see Him or touch Him in a physical way, but we have the sense that He has appeared to us. Unable to deny the sense that

God has appeared to us, we will want to worship and adore Him, offering to Him our praise and thanksgiving. This is the experience of the appearing of God to us as the result of our priestly service. We should have such an experience not only early in the morning but also during the day.

We may experience God's appearing to us in different situations. For example, we may enjoy God's appearing while we are preaching the gospel. In our gospel preaching we may apply Christ as the offerings, and as a result we enjoy the appearing of God to us. Often we have this enjoyment in the church meetings. God may appear to us even as we are taking a walk.

Our New Testament priesthood issues in the enjoyment of God in His appearing. Usually God's appearing will be tranquil and cause us to be silent. Sometimes God will sovereignly arrange our circumstances to match the tranquility of His appearing. At such times it seems that the entire universe is quiet and that we and God are alone. This tranquil appearing of God is the first result of our New Testament priestly service.

II. THE APPEARING OF GOD'S GLORY TO US

The second issue of the priestly service is the appearing of God's glory to us. When we serve God in our spirit by enjoying Christ according to God's regulations, we will enjoy God's appearing, which is often followed by the appearing of God's glory. God's glory is God expressed. When God is expressed, that is glory.

When we serve God with Christ as the offerings according to God's regulations and not according to our own choice, we will often enjoy the appearing of God's glory. We will see God expressed in different ways. For example, when we enter the home of an unbeliever for the preaching of the gospel, we may sense God's glory manifested in our speaking or in his expression or attitude toward us. Furthermore, we often enjoy God's glory, His expression, in the church meetings. Perhaps a particular meeting is not very living, but then someone offers a living prayer, and the meeting is resurrected and revived.

At such a time we may sense that God is expressed in glory.

In 2 Corinthians 3 Paul wrote concerning the glory of the Old Testament ministry and the glory of the New Testament ministry. "Now if the ministry of death, in letters engraved in stone, came in glory, so that the sons of Israel were not able to gaze at the face of Moses because of the glory of his face, which was being done away, how shall not rather the ministry of the Spirit be in glory? For if the ministry of condemnation came in glory, much rather the ministry of righteousness abounds in glory" (vv. 7-9). With Moses, who had the Old Testament ministry of death and condemnation, there was a glory, a physical glory, on his face. We who have the ministry of the New Testament, of the Spirit and of righteousness, have a glory in life and in spirit.

The Christian meeting is wonderful and mysterious because it is related to God. The Lord Jesus said, "Where two or three are gathered together in My name, there I am in their midst" (Matt. 18:20). We believe that the Lord is with us in every meeting, but He is present in different ways and, depending on our situation in the meetings, He causes us to have different kinds of senses regarding the meeting. For instance, on one occasion He may cause us to have a sense of deadness to indicate that our situation is wrong. On another occasion He may stir up everyone in the meeting, and all the attendants will have the sense that God is stirring them up. This kind of stirring up is altogether divine, and in it God appears to us in His glory, in His expression.

The appearing of God's glory in the church meetings is related to our enjoyment of Christ as the offerings. If in a church of two hundred saints, sixty would enjoy Christ as the offerings all day, in the evening when they come together, the appearing of God and the very expression of God would be among them. Their coming together into the name of Christ is the expression of God. However, the situation would be the opposite if none of the saints enjoyed Christ as the offerings. Their coming together would not be the expression of God.

The atmosphere of the meetings indicates what we are with God. No one can pretend. The meeting is truly an exhibition of our Christian life, in particular, of the degree to which we enjoy Christ in our private daily life and in our family life. Our meeting is an exhibition of our actual enjoyment of Christ. If we enjoy Christ, the meeting will be an exhibition of the riches of Christ. If we do not enjoy Christ, there will not be an exhibition of the riches of Christ in the meeting. In this matter shouting and praising do not help, for the meeting is not under our control. The point here is that our experience of Christ affects the meetings; it especially affects, even determines, the atmosphere of the church meetings.

The atmosphere of the meetings is an indication of the appearing of God's glory, and this appearing depends on the ministering of Christ as the offerings. When we minister Christ as the different offerings, we enjoy Him, and those to whom we minister also enjoy Him. This will affect the atmosphere of the meetings because it will issue in the appearing of God's glory to us.

III. AARON BLESSING THE PEOPLE

Leviticus 9:22 says, "Then Aaron lifted up his hands toward the people and blessed them; and he came down from offering the sin offering, the burnt offering, and the peace offerings." This signifies that Christ as our High Priest after His crucifixion blessed us in His resurrection (Luke 24:50).

The Lord in His resurrection is with us all the days until the consummation of the age (Matt. 28:20). The Lord's presence with us is His blessing. As long as we have His presence, we are under His blessing. When His blessing is with us, even our mistakes become blessings. But without His presence, even if we are right in everything, there is nothing but vanity. Although our High Priest has gone into the heavens, He is still present with us, and His presence is a blessing not only in the church life but also in our family life and in our practical daily life.

The Lord's presence as our blessing comes to us through

our application of Him as all the offerings. Every day we need to apply Christ as our sin offering, burnt offering, meal offering, and peace offering. If we apply Him as these offerings, we will have His blessing, which is His presence.

John 3:16 says that God so loved the world that He gave His only begotten Son. In what way did God give His Son to us? He gave Him to us as all the offerings. When we take the sin offering, we take an aspect of Christ. When we take the burnt offering, we take another aspect of Christ. When we take the meal offering and the peace offering, we take yet other aspects of Christ.

Our Savior is the unique sin offering. When we repented and believed in the Lord Jesus, we applied Him as the sin offering without realizing it. Later, we might have been inspired to be absolute for God. Although we had not heard about the burnt offering, we prayed and offered ourselves to God. At that time, the Spirit might have shown us that we are sin, even leprous, and that we cannot be absolute for God. Then we might have prayed, "Lord Jesus, I cannot be absolute for God, but You are absolute, and You can be my absoluteness." This is to take Christ, the Son given to us by God, as the burnt offering.

Many Christians understand John 3:16 in a very general way. How can we accept Christ as the great gift from God if we do not apply Christ as the offerings? If we would enjoy this all-inclusive person, we need to apply Him daily as our sin offering, burnt offering, meal offering, and peace offering. Then we will enjoy His presence as our blessing in every way.

IV. MOSES AND AARON ENTERING INTO THE TENT OF MEETING AND COMING OUT TO BLESS THE PEOPLE

"Moses and Aaron went into the tent of meeting, and when they came out they blessed the people" (Lev. 9:23a). This signifies that Christ as our Prince and High Priest entered into the heavens to be our kingly Priest (Acts 5:31; Heb. 4:14; 7:1) and will come out of the heavens to bless us.

Both Moses and Aaron typify Christ. Moses was the

leader, the prince, and Aaron was the high priest. Today Christ is our Prince and our High Priest. When He comes to us, He comes with blessings, and His being with us is the all-inclusive blessing we need. We can enjoy this blessing only by applying Christ as the offerings. If we apply Him as the sin offering, the burnt offering, the meal offering, and the peace offering, we will have the blessing we need.

The blessing of Aaron and Moses upon the Jews is still in effect. This blessing will continue until the entire house of Israel repents and turns to the Savior at His second coming. The principle is the same with the spiritual blessing we enjoy today. A spiritual blessing lasts much longer than we realize. I am still enjoying certain blessings which I received many years ago. A spiritual blessing, therefore, is a great matter.

The New Testament tells us to bless others and not to curse them (Luke 6:28; Rom. 12:14). Even if we are hated, persecuted, and evilly spoken of, we should bless those who persecute us and pray that the Lord will forgive them. In our feeling, no person should be under a curse.

V. FIRE COMING OUT FROM GOD
AND CONSUMING THE BURNT OFFERING

"Then fire came out from before Jehovah and consumed the burnt offering and the portions of fat on the altar; and when all the people saw it, they shouted and fell on their faces" (Lev. 9:24). This fire signifies that God's holiness as a consuming fire accepts our offerings by burning. Anything that corresponds to God's holy nature God's holiness accepts by consuming it. But anything that does not meet the requirements of God's holiness will be judged by God's holiness through burning. In such a case, the fire represents the God who is the consuming fire (Heb. 12:29).

After we enjoy God's presence, the appearing of His glory, and the Lord's blessing, we should be prepared to receive the consuming fire. It is a spiritual law that God's blessing is followed by the consuming fire of suffering.

This fire is a sign that God has accepted what we have offered to Him in Christ and with Christ.

The same fire, which is the representative of God's holiness, may either be a consuming fire for God's acceptance or a judging fire. The consuming fire accepted the offering up of Stephen (Acts 7:55-59), whereas with the coming of Titus in A.D. 70 this consuming fire judged the mixture at Jerusalem.

To us today, the consuming fire may be a divine acceptance of our offering to God, or it may be God's judgment due to our offenses. How do we know whether the consuming fire is God's acceptance or God's judgment? This can be discerned by our situation. If we enjoy Christ and offer Him to God, the consuming fire will be God's acceptance. However, if we offend God's government and a burning comes to us, this burning is God's judgment upon us for touching His government. This is a serious matter.

LIFE-STUDY OF LEVITICUS

PART ONE—MESSAGE THIRTY-THREE

THE LESSON AND
THE REGULATIONS FOR THE PRIESTS

(1)

Scripture Reading: Lev. 10:1-11

In chapters one through nine of Leviticus, we have seen the offerings and their laws, the consecration of Aaron and his sons, the initiation of the priestly service, and the issue of the priestly service. The issue of the priestly service includes the appearing of God, the appearing of God's glory, the blessing of the people, and fire coming out from before God and consuming the burnt offering (9:24). This consuming fire, which represents God's holiness, is used by God in two different kinds of situations, one positive and the other negative. In a positive situation, when we have something for God and offer it to God, He accepts it by consuming it with fire. This consuming is positive; it is the divine acceptance of what we are, what we do, and what we have for God. In a negative situation, holy fire comes from God as judgment. Such a negative case—the case of Nadab and Abihu—is found in Leviticus 10:1-11, the section which we will consider in this message.

The case of Nadab and Abihu in 10:1-11 goes together with the events of the previous chapter. It seems that this sad case happened on the same day in which "fire came out from before Jehovah and consumed the burnt offering and the portions of fat on the altar" (9:24).

Nadab and Abihu, sons of Aaron, did something that seemingly was good: they offered something to God. However, they offered "strange fire" (10:1), common fire, not fire from the heavens. God judged this offering of strange fire by consuming the two priests who offered it.

This shows us, on the one hand, that God is merciful and kind, and, on the other hand, that He is quite severe and strict. After the blessings of that excellent and glorious day in chapter nine, the day of God's initiation of the application of Christ to His people for their enjoyment, we might have tolerated the mistake recorded in chapter ten. But with God there was no tolerance. Immediately after God blessed, He judged.

The consuming of the offerings by the heavenly fire was altogether positive. That consuming was a strong confirmation that God is the true and living God and that He was with His people, the people of Israel. Furthermore, this consuming by fire was a confirmation of what Moses had done and of what he had told the people about God. Before that time, the Israelites might have wondered what kind of God they had, for they had heard about Him through Moses, but they had not seen Him. Now there was a particular day with all kinds of laws, regulations, and offerings, a day that was formal and official. On this day God's glory appeared, and His blessing came upon His people. Furthermore, on this day there was the divine acceptance of the offerings. This acceptance came in the form of consuming fire. This fire came down from heaven; it was not from the earth, and it did not originate with the children of Israel. When fire came from heaven to the very spot—the altar—where the offerings were and consumed the offerings, the people saw it, shouted, and fell on their faces (9:24b).

Not long afterward, the consuming fire appeared again but in a negative way. Instead of accepting, the holy fire judged. In chapter nine the holy fire consumed in the sense of accepting; in chapter ten the holy fire consumed in the sense of judging. Concerning Nadab and Abihu, 10:2 says, "Fire came out from before Jehovah and consumed them, and they died before Jehovah." A similar thing occurred in Acts. On the day of Pentecost the glory of God came down from heaven (Acts 2:1-4), but not long afterward a couple cheated the Holy Spirit and died as a result (Acts 5:1-11). In the case in Leviticus 10, the offering of something not sanctified, a common, worldly fire, brought in judgment. The holy, heavenly fire consumed Nadab and Abihu, and they died.

The more we consider the case of Nadab and Abihu, the more we realize that God is not only merciful but also holy, not only kind but also severe. Therefore, we should not be careless in serving Him or in touching the divine things.

Leviticus 10:9 and 10 say, "Do not drink wine or strong drink, you or your sons with you, when you come into the tent of meeting, that you may not die; it is a perpetual statute throughout your generations, that you may make a distinction between the holy and the common, and between the unclean and the clean." This charge indicates that the reason Nadab and Abihu offered strange fire might have been that they were drunk with wine. This made them loose and careless and caused them to act without fear. As a result, they suffered God's holy judgment.

In both the Old Testament and the New Testament, the principle is the same concerning the result of carelessness in serving God and in touching the divine things. In the case both of Nadab and Abihu and of Ananias and Sapphira the result was death. This shows us that the careless touching of the divine things is serious and may result in death. According to the New Testament, this death may not be physical but spiritual.

Let us now consider in some detail the case of Nadab and Abihu.

I. THE LESSON OF NADAB AND ABIHU

In 10:1-11 we have the lesson of Nadab and Abihu. The consuming of Nadab and Abihu probably took place at the end of the day of glory and blessing described in chapter nine. What happened to these two sons of Aaron is surely a lesson for us today.

A. Nadab and Abihu
Offering Strange Fire before Jehovah

"The sons of Aaron, Nadab and Abihu, each took his censer and put fire in it, and placed incense upon it, and offered strange fire before Jehovah, which He had not commanded them" (v. 1). This signifies man's natural enthusiasm, natural affection, natural strength, and natural ability offered to God.

Nadab and Abihu were not judged because they did something that was not for God. They were judged because they acted according to the natural life. They did something for God, but they did it in a natural way. They might have loved God, but they loved Him in a natural way.

We should be burning for the Lord and hot; however, our hotness should not be natural but spiritual. We progress from being natural to being spiritual by taking the way of the cross. Whatever we are in the natural life should be crossed out. The natural man has already been crucified with Christ. Now in our Christian life and walk we need to hold the attitude that our natural man has been crucified and must be set aside. Since the natural life has already been condemned, we should condemn it today. We need to realize that our natural man has been judged by God on the cross, and for this reason it should not be regarded or honored.

Our serving in the church and our testifying in the meetings can easily be natural. If we speak in the meetings in a natural way, we will offer strange, or common, fire, and this will bring in spiritual death. Whenever we testify in a natural way, our being is deadened, and the meeting with its atmosphere also is deadened.

We all need to learn not to touch the holy things of God with the natural life. Not only should the things be right, but the way should also be right. It is not adequate simply to do the right thing. We must do the right thing in the right way. To offer strange fire to God is to do the right thing in the wrong way, and this brings in the judgment of death.

It is not easy to be purified from being natural. We may often exercise our natural enthusiasm, natural affection, natural strength, or natural ability. Everything natural in us needs to be dealt with.

The life of Moses is an illustration of dealing with the natural man. Moses said that "the days of our years are threescore years and ten" and that "by reason of strength" they may be fourscore years (Psa. 90:10). According to his understanding, the age of eighty marks the end of man's life. It is significant, therefore, that Moses was called by God when he was eighty years old. This indicates that Moses' natural life had come to an end and that whatever he did for God was in resurrection. At the age of eighty Moses had a new beginning, and from then on he did not act according to his natural life but according to a resurrection spirit.

Regardless of our age, we all need to learn not to do or say things with the natural strength, by the natural ability, or for the natural affection. We must regard everything natural as a snake, a poison.

The fire offered by Nadab and Abihu was common fire; it was not fire from the altar. The fire from the altar, having touched the offerings, was holy and also sanctified. However, Nadab and Abihu did not offer such a sanctified and sanctifying fire but a common fire. This fire was not from Jehovah but from man; it was not from the heavens but from the earth, and it had no base of propitiation. Without propitiation the situation between man and God cannot be appeased. Rather, the problems between man and God remain.

Due to the influence of Catholicism and Protestantism, many Christians today are loose and careless concerning the worship and service of God. They do not take this worship and service seriously, and the result is the exercise of the natural life issuing in spiritual death.

B. Fire Coming Out from before Jehovah and Consuming Them to Death before Jehovah

Leviticus 10:2 tells us that "fire came out from before Jehovah" and consumed Nadab and Abihu, and "they died before Jehovah." This fire is the opposite of common fire. This fire is from God, not from man; it is from the heavens, not from the earth; and it is for judgment, not for acceptance.

The fire in verse 2 is also fire for the sanctification of God by His serving ones who come near to Him (v. 3a). The

death of Nadab and Abihu sanctified God. Their death
tells us that God is not common but holy and that we
should not offer anything common to this holy God. From
the death of Nadab and Abihu we learn that God must be
honored as a holy God. If we are not serious with Him, we
will be judged, and His judgment upon us will be His
sanctification of Himself.

The fire in verse 2 was also for the glorification of God
before His people (v. 3b). Aaron and the people might have
felt that this consuming fire was only a matter of
punishment and judgment, but with God this fire was a
matter of His glorification.

C. The Corpses of Nadab and Abihu
Being Carried Away from the Front
of the Holy Place outside the Camp

"Moses called Mishael and Elzaphan, the sons of
Uzziel, the uncle of Aaron, and said to them, Come near;
carry your brothers away from the front of the holy place
outside the camp. So they came near and carried them
in their tunics outside the camp, as Moses had spoken"
(vv. 4-5). This signifies that the deadness of unholiness
should be kept away from the sphere of God's holiness and
also from the community, the fellowship, of God's people.

D. The Priests Not Disheveling Their Hair
nor Tearing Their Garments over
God's Death-judgment upon Their Relatives,
That They May Not Die and That
God May Not Be Angry with All the Congregation

"Moses said to Aaron, and to Eleazar and to Ithamar,
his sons, Do not dishevel your hair nor tear your garments,
that you may not die and that He may not be angry with
all the congregation" (v. 6). This signifies that even God's
death-judgment upon the relatives should not be an excuse
for His serving ones to be disorderly in their subjection to
the headship of Christ and to break the perfection of their
conduct, that they might not suffer deadness in their
spiritual life and cause God to be unhappy with His people.

The requirement in verse 6 indicates that we must mean business with God. In coming to Him and in touching His service and work, we must be serious. Even if relatives are lost due to God's death-judgment, we must take care of God's concern and not our own concern. Behaving in such a situation as though we have suffered no loss shows that we are under the headship of Christ.

E. The Whole House of Israel
Bewailing the Burning Which Jehovah Has Kindled

Leviticus 10:6c says, "But let your brothers, the whole house of Israel, bewail the burning which Jehovah has kindled." This signifies that the whole body of God's people should grieve over the judgment of God upon the unholiness of His serving ones.

F. The Priests Not Going Out
from the Entrance of the Tent of Meeting
So That They May Not Die,
for the Anointing Oil of Jehovah Is upon Them

"And you shall not go out from the entrance of the tent of meeting so that you may not die, for the anointing oil of Jehovah is upon you" (v. 7a). The priests could not leave the entrance of the tent of meeting even to attend the funeral, because the holy anointing oil, which typifies the processed Triune God, was upon them. This signifies that God's serving ones, bearing the Holy Spirit of God, should not leave the entering in of the church life that they may not suffer spiritual deadness.

G. The Priests Not Drinking Any Wine
When They Come into the Tent of Meeting
That They May Not Die, and That They May Make
a Distinction between the Holy and the Common,
between the Unclean and the Clean,
and That They May Teach the People
All the Statutes of Jehovah

"Jehovah spoke to Aaron, saying, Do not drink wine or strong drink, you or your sons with you, when you come into the tent of meeting, that you may not die; it is a perpetual statute throughout your generations, that you may make a distinction between the holy and the common, and between the unclean and the clean, and that you may teach the sons of Israel all the statutes which Jehovah has spoken to them through Moses" (vv. 8-11). This signifies that God's serving ones coming into the church life should not drink anything of the worldly enjoyment, of the fleshly interest, and of the natural excitement that they might not suffer spiritual deadness but be able to make a distinction between the holy and the common and between the clean and the unclean, and to teach God's people His regulations.

If we pay attention to the lesson of Nadab and Abihu, we will learn a great deal. Surely this lesson will then govern us in touching the things concerning God.

LIFE-STUDY OF LEVITICUS

THE LESSON AND
THE REGULATIONS FOR THE PRIESTS

(2)

Scripture Reading: Lev. 10:12-20

In the foregoing message we covered the lesson for the priests. In this message we will consider the regulations for the priests.

II. THE REGULATIONS FOR THE PRIESTS

Although on a day of glory, a day full of blessing and enjoyment, something severe happened to Aaron (10:1-11), in 10:12 we have a further expression of God's mercy and grace. "Moses spoke to Aaron, and to Eleazar and to Ithamar, his sons who remained, Take the meal offering that remains of the offerings of Jehovah by fire and eat it unleavened beside the altar, for it is most holy." This verse speaks not of the burnt offering, the sin offering, or the trespass offering but the meal offering. The meal offering here is a matter of God's mercy and grace. To our thought, immediately after the correction in 10:1-11, Aaron and his sons needed a sin offering. But Moses told them to eat the meal offering. Something was presented to Aaron and his sons for their eating. To give others something to eat at the time of need is to show them mercy.

The holy fire that consumed Nadab and Abihu was for judgment. This judgment was exercised not on unbelievers but on God's people. According to 1 Corinthians 11:27-32, this kind of judgment is a disciplinary punishment, a merciful correction, not a judgment for perdition. The judgment of God on Aaron's two sons did not terminate God's mercy on His people. As Leviticus 10:12 indicates, here God's mercy went along with His punishment and correction.

A. Aaron and His Sons Eating
the Remainder of the Meal Offering,
of the Offerings of Jehovah by Fire,
without Leaven in a Holy Place
beside the Altar, as Their Portion

Aaron and his sons ate the remainder of the meal offering, of the offerings of Jehovah by fire, without leaven in a holy place beside the altar, as their portion (vv. 12-13). This signifies that the remaining part of Christ in His humanity as our meal offering is for us, the New Testament priests, to enjoy as our portion. According to Leviticus 2, the top portion of the meal offering, with the frankincense, was to be offered to God by fire. The remainder of the meal offering was for the priests. As the meal offering, Christ is firstly for God's satisfaction, and then He is for our enjoyment and satisfaction.

Once again I would emphasize the fact that the meal offering in verses 12 and 13 comes immediately after the disciplinary judgment upon Nadab and Abihu and indicates that God is merciful. After this death-judgment Moses did not say, "Aaron, you have made mistakes, and now is the time for you to offer a sin offering to God." Rather, instead of telling Aaron and his sons to offer a sin offering or a burnt offering, Moses told them to eat the remainder of the meal offering. This indicates that the judging and correcting God continues to be merciful.

The meal offering, which was most holy, was to be eaten in a holy place, that is, in a place where God is. This means that the meal offering was to be eaten in God's presence. Furthermore, it was to be eaten beside the cross (the altar). Without the cross we have no position to enjoy anything of Christ. Also, the meal offering was to be eaten without sin (unleavened) as an offering that could be accepted by God in the fire of His holiness.

B. The Breast of the People's Peace
Offerings as the Wave Offering and
the Thigh as the Heave Offering Offered
to Jehovah with the Offerings by Fire
of the Portions of Fat Being Eaten
by the Priests in a Clean Place

The breast of the people's peace offerings as the wave
offering and the thigh of the heave offering offered to
Jehovah with the offerings by fire of the portions of fat
were to be eaten by the priests in a clean place (vv. 14-15).
This signifies that we, the New Testament priests, share
with God some aspects of Christ as the believers' peace
offering.

The breast of the wave offering signifies the loving
capacity of Christ in His resurrection. Christ has the
particular capacity to love with God's love. His loving
capacity is not in the natural life but in resurrection.

The thigh of the heave offering signifies Christ's
strengthening power in His ascension. The strongest parts
of our physical body are the thighs. They have not only the
standing power but also the strengthening power. Today
Christ is strengthening us in His ascension.

The breast and the thigh were to be eaten in a clean
place, signifying a clean condition apart from sin or any
negative thing. Furthermore, they were to be eaten as an
offering that could be accepted by God in the fire of His
holiness.

C. The Sin Offering Which Is Most
Holy and the Blood of Which Was Not
Brought into the Holy of Holies,
Being Eaten by the Priests in the Holy Place
That They Might Bear Away
the Iniquity of the Congregation
to Make Propitiation for Them before Jehovah

The sin offering which was most holy and the blood of
which was not brought into the Holy of Holies was eaten
by the priests in the holy place that they might bear away
the iniquity of the congregation to make propitiation for

them before Jehovah (vv. 17b-18). This signifies that we, the New Testament priests, partake of Christ as the believers' sin offering. This partaking is in the sense of participating in Christ's life, the life that bears others' sins, as our life supply, that we may be able to bear the problems of God's people. We partake of this offering in the church life in order to minister Christ's sin-dealing life to the believers that they may deal with their sins. The goal of such a dealing is to appease the situation of the believers with God and to restore their broken fellowship with God.

Verse 17 speaks of making propitiation for the people. The word *propitiation* in the Old Testament does not refer to the redemption accomplished and completed by Christ. Rather, propitiation in the Old Testament is a type pointing to the redemption of Christ.

The Hebrew word translated "make propitiation" is *kaphar*, which means "to cover." The noun form of this word is rendered "propitiatory cover" in 16:2, 13-15, and refers to the lid of the ark of the testimony. When someone came to contact God, immediately the Ten Commandments within the ark in the Holy of Holies exposed his sinful condition, indicating that there was a problem between this sinful person and the righteous God. Thus, there was no peace between these two parties. However, the blood of the sin offering was sprinkled upon the lid that covered the ark, signifying that the sin of the one coming to contact God had been covered.

In the Old Testament time Christ had not yet come, but there was a type pointing to Christ. That type was the animal sacrifice which was offered to God as a sin offering. On the day of propitiation the animal was slain, and its shed blood was brought into the Holy of Holies and sprinkled on the lid of the ark. In this way the problem between God and man was covered but not settled. This covering temporarily satisfied God's requirement. This is to propitiate, to appease, to do something for the owing party to satisfy the requiring party, producing peace between the two parties.

Hebrews 9:12 clearly speaks of Christ's redemption, telling us that "through His own blood" Christ has "entered once for all into the Holy of Holies, having found an eternal redemption." The accomplished and completed redemption of Christ was obtained when He brought His blood to the heavens and sprinkled it there. In this way Christ found, obtained, procured, redemption. Redemption was accomplished by Christ on the cross, and it was obtained by Christ the Redeemer from the hand of the redeeming God. What we receive today is not merely propitiation or some kind of appeasing but the accomplished and completed redemption. Now we are enjoying such a redemption.

Leviticus 10:17 and 18 indicate that we, the New Testament priests, partake of Christ as the believers' sin offering in the sense of participating in Christ's life, the life that bears others' sins, as our life supply, that we may be able to bear the problems of God's people. If we would take Christ as the sin offering, we need to realize that after eating such a Christ we should bear the problems of God's people.

Eating is not only for satisfaction; it is also for working (2 Thes. 3:10). If we eat Christ as our sin offering, the offering that has accomplished redemption for us and has solved our problems with God, we must bear the responsibility to solve the problems of God's people.

If you become aware that a certain brother has a problem with sin, you should first bear the burden to pray for him. Then according to the Spirit's leading, you may go to visit him, not to condemn him or to point out his failure but to fellowship with him to bring him into the presence of the Lord and into the sense of the Lord's mercy and grace. If you can bring him into the light of God, the light will shine upon him and within him, and he will see his sinfulness, mistakes, and shortcomings.

Do not try to help a sinful one by exposing him or by directly pointing out his shortcomings. If you do this, you will insult him. Every sinner holds to his prestige. If you point out a brother's sin, he will not confess it but will hold to his prestige. Furthermore, instead of bringing the brother into the light, you will provoke him and cause problems.

The best way to help a sinful brother is to be a person who lives in the fellowship of the Lord. Then when you visit such a one, you will bear with you an atmosphere of fellowship, and you will bring that one into fellowship with the enlightening God. In this fellowship he will be enlightened and will touch God's mercy and grace. The mercy and grace of the divine life will soften his hard heart and warm his cold heart. (Because sinning causes one's heart to become hard and cold, the heart of a sinful brother needs to be softened and warmed.) In the softening and warming light of God, the brother will see his sinfulness and confess it. There will be no need for you to mention it. This way of helping a sinful brother is the way of love in wisdom.

If we would bear the problems of God's people, we need to have a rich enjoyment of Christ as our sin offering. Then with much prayer and consideration we should contact others in love and with wisdom, ministering Christ's sin-dealing life to them that they may deal with their sins. If we contact others in this way, we will not damage them or the church but rather will do something to bear the problems of God's people.

D. Due to the Weakness concerning God's Death-judgment upon Nadab and Abihu, Aaron and His Sons Being Not Fit to Eat the Sin Offering

Due to his weakness concerning God's death-judgment upon Nadab and Abihu, Aaron and his sons were not fit to eat the sin offering (Lev. 10:16-17a, 19-20). This signifies that if we are weak in accepting God's judgment upon the serving ones who are intimate and close to us, we will not be able to partake of Christ as our sin offering in the sense of taking His sin-dealing life as our life supply to minister Him to the believers as the sin-dealing life.

"Moses diligently inquired about the goat of the sin

offering, and found that it had been burned up! And he was angry with Eleazar and Ithamar, Aaron's sons who remained, and said, Why have you not eaten the sin offering in the holy place?" (vv. 16-17a). Since the blood of this sin offering had not been brought inside, into the holy place, they should have eaten it as Moses had commanded (v. 18). Moses therefore rebuked them for not doing so. Then Aaron said to Moses, "See, today they have offered their sin offering and their burnt offering before Jehovah, and such things as these have happened to me! If I had eaten the sin offering today, would it be pleasing in the sight of Jehovah?" (v. 19). On the one hand, Aaron and his sons were weak concerning God's death-judgment; on the other hand, Aaron had a proper consideration, for he and his sons were sorrowful and unhappy, and eating the sin offering under such circumstances would not have been pleasing to the Lord. Aaron told Moses that because of their sorrow, it would not have been fitting for them to eat the sin offering. "When Moses heard that, it was pleasing in his sight" (v. 20). Aaron's response pleased Moses, who represented God, and thus God also must have been pleased.

This incident indicates that with respect to keeping the regulations made by God, in God's mercy there is a margin that is out of consideration for our circumstances. Aaron and his sons had not kept God's regulation in a legal way. They had not followed the divine regulation, not because of disobedience but because of a positive consideration of their circumstances.

These verses also show us that we should not keep God's regulations in a rushed way. Instead of following the divine regulation in a hurried way, Aaron and his sons considered their situation and circumstances, and thus did not keep the regulation legally. What Aaron and his sons did was seemingly against God's regulation, but actually it was something done in wisdom.

LIFE-STUDY OF LEVITICUS

PART ONE — MESSAGE THIRTY-FIVE

A CONCLUDING WORD ON THE OFFERINGS
AND THE PRIESTHOOD

Scripture Reading: Heb. 1:2-3; 2:14; 3:1; 4:14-15; 6:20; 7:22,
25-26; 8:1-2; 9:11-12, 24-28; 10:5-7, 9-10, 19-21; 12:2, 24; 13:21

This message, which will focus on Hebrews as an
exposition of Leviticus, is a concluding word to all the
foregoing messages on the offerings and the priesthood.

THE ALL-INCLUSIVE CHRIST
AS HE IS REVEALED IN HEBREWS

In the book of Hebrews there are many references to the
book of Leviticus, especially to the offerings and the
priesthood. For example, Leviticus often speaks of the high
priest. No other New Testament book speaks as much
about Christ as the High Priest than the book of Hebrews
does.

In the book of Leviticus itself we cannot see how great,
excellent, wonderful, all-inclusive, and inexhaustible is the
Christ whom we offer and enjoy as the offerings. In
Leviticus we can see that all the offerings typify Christ,
but we do not get the realization and the sense of how
great Christ is. No word can express the greatness of the
Christ who is all the offerings.

For a revelation of the all-inclusiveness of Christ, we
need to come to the book of Hebrews. Let us now briefly
survey the aspects of Christ revealed in Hebrews.

The Creator, the Upholder, and the Heir

Hebrews 1:2 and 3 tell us that Christ is the Maker, the
Creator, of the universe and that He is also the Upholder of
the universe He created. Furthermore, God has appointed
Christ to be the Heir of all things of the universe.

The Effulgence of God's Glory
and the Express Image of His Substance

In verse 3 we see that Christ is the effulgence of God's glory and the express image of His substance. The effulgence of God's glory is like the shining or brightness of the light of the sun. Christ is the shining, the brightness, of the Father's glory. The express image of God's substance is like the impress of a seal. Christ the Son is the expression of what God the Father is.

The One Who Has Destroyed the Devil

"Since therefore the children have partaken of blood and flesh, He also Himself in like manner shared in the same, that through death He might destroy him who has the might of death, that is, the Devil" (2:14). The wonderful One, who is the Maker of the universe, partook of blood and flesh in order to destroy the Devil, to bring him to naught. In the fullness of time, the Son of God came to become flesh (John 1:14; Rom. 8:3) by being born of a virgin (Gal. 4:4), that He might destroy the Devil in man's flesh through His death on the cross.

The Apostle and the High Priest

In Hebrews 3:1 we see that Christ is "the Apostle and High Priest of our confession." As the Apostle, Christ is the One sent to us from God and with God. As the High Priest, Christ is the One who went back to God from us and with us. As the Apostle, Christ came to us with God to share God with us that we may partake of the divine life, nature, and fullness. As the High Priest, Christ went to God with us to present us to God that we and all our case may be fully cared for by Him. Thus, 4:14 and 15 say, "Having therefore a great High Priest who has passed through the heavens, Jesus, the Son of God, let us hold fast the confession. For we do not have a high priest who is not able to sympathize with our weaknesses, but One who has been tried in all respects like us, yet without sin." As such a High Priest, Christ bears us in the presence of God and cares for all our needs.

The Forerunner

Hebrews 6:20 reveals that Christ is our Forerunner. The Lord Jesus as the Forerunner took the lead to pass through the stormy sea and to enter into the heavenly haven, "into that which is within the veil" (v. 19), to be the High Priest for us according to the order of Melchisedec, the order of the priesthood that is in both humanity and divinity. As the Forerunner, He has cut the way into glory.

The Surety of a Better Covenant

"By so much also Jesus has become the surety of a better covenant" (7:22). In this verse Christ is the surety of a better covenant. Christ's being the surety of a better covenant is based on His being the living and perpetual High Priest. The word *surety* here means that Christ has pledged Himself to the new covenant and to all of us. He is the bondsman, the guarantee that He will do everything necessary for the fulfillment of the new covenant.

The High Priest Who Is
Able to Save Us to the Uttermost

"Wherefore also He is able to save to the uttermost those who come forward to God through Him, seeing He is always living to intercede for them. For such a High Priest befits us, holy, guileless, undefiled, separated from sinners, and become higher than the heavens" (7:25-26). Having passed through the heavens (4:14) and even being higher than the heavens (7:26), the Lord Jesus is always living to intercede for us. Christ as our High Priest undertakes our case by interceding for us. He appears before God on our behalf, praying for us that we may be saved and brought fully into God's eternal purpose.

The Minister in the Heavens

"We have such a High Priest, who sat down on the right hand of the throne of the Majesty in the heavens, a Minister of the holy places, even of the true tabernacle, which the Lord pitched, not man" (8:1-2). The heavenly Christ is ministering in a tabernacle pitched by the Lord and not by man. This tabernacle, this sanctuary, is in the third heaven, in which is the heavenly Holy of Holies. Christ, as a Minister of the true (heavenly) tabernacle, ministers heaven (which is not only a place but a condition of life) into us, so that we may live a heavenly life on earth as He did while He was here.

The One Who Entered into the Holy of Holies in the Heavens and Obtained an Eternal Redemption

"Christ having come a High Priest of the good things that have come, through the greater and more perfect tabernacle not made by hand, that is, not of this creation, nor through the blood of goats and calves, but through His own blood, entered once for all into the Holy of Holies, having found an eternal redemption" (9:11-12). Since Christ as the Lamb of God took away the sin of the world (John 1:29) by offering Himself on the cross as the sacrifice for sins once for all (Heb. 9:14; 10:12), His blood, which He sprinkled in the heavenly tabernacle, has accomplished an eternal redemption for us. Through this, Christ "found an eternal redemption." Here the word *found* really means obtained, procured. By sprinkling His blood in the heavens before God, Christ has found, obtained, procured, eternal redemption for us.

The One Appearing before God for Us

Christ appeared the first time to take away our sin and our sins, and He will appear a second time apart from sin (9:24-28). Hebrews 9:24 says that Christ is now appearing "before the face of God for us." He "has been manifested for the putting away of sin by His sacrifice" (v. 26b). This indicates that He is the sin offering. Verse 28 goes on to say that He has been "once offered to bear the sins of many." This indicates that He is also the trespass offering.

The Replacement of the Old Testament Offerings

Hebrews 10:5-10 tells us that when Christ came, God had no more desire for or pleasure and interest in the animal sacrifices (vv. 6, 8). Christ's coming annulled the Levitical offerings. Nevertheless, the significance of all these offerings remains with Christ.

God prepared a human body for Christ, the incarnated God-man (v. 5), so that He could be the replacement of all the Old Testament offerings. By replacing the offerings of the first covenant with Himself, Christ did the will of God (vv. 7, 9), taking away the first, the offerings of the Old Testament, and establishing the second, Himself as the reality of all those offerings.

In Leviticus we have the first category of the offerings. As the replacement of these offerings, Christ is the second category of offerings. He is now the burnt offering, the meal offering, the peace offering, the sin offering, and the trespass offering. He is also the wave offering, the heave offering, the consecration offering, the freewill offering, and the offering for thanksgiving. Therefore, God no longer has any pleasure in the sacrifices of the first covenant. Today God's pleasure is only in a unique person—Jesus Christ. He, the all-inclusive Christ, is all the offerings.

CHRIST, OUR PERPETUAL DUE

All the aspects of Christ revealed in Hebrews are inexhaustible. He is the Creator, the Upholder, the Heir, the One who has destroyed the Devil, the Apostle, the High Priest, the Forerunner, the Surety, the heavenly Minister, the One appearing before God on our behalf, and the replacement of all the Old Testament offerings. Christ is the reality of every positive thing (Col. 2:16-17), including you and me (Phil. 1:21; Gal. 2:20).

Such a wonderful Christ is our perpetual due. This means that the all-inclusive Christ is our eternal portion for us to enjoy. We not only offer Christ to God—we also enjoy Him as we offer Him to God. We thus enjoy Christ with God, for we and God are co-eaters, eating Christ together in fellowship. This enjoyment is marvelous, and it is impossible for human words to describe it adequately.

CHRIST, THE GIFT WE HAVE RECEIVED FROM GOD

Christ is God's gift to us. "God so loved the world that He gave His only begotten Son" (John 3:16). In the offerings, Christ is also the gift we offer to God. (The Hebrew for offering in Leviticus 1:2, *corban*, means a gift or present.) What gift could be greater than Christ? Christ is surely the greatest gift!

We enjoy Christ as God's gift in the "gift shop" of the church. Every local church is a gift shop displaying Christ. This unique gift has thousands of aspects. Just as a diamond has many facets, so Christ has a great many facets. In one facet He is the Father, while in another facet He is the Son.

Enjoying Christ in His aspects and facets is for our worship of God; it is also for our fellowship with Him and with one another and for our eating in our daily living. Worship that is humanly manufactured is an abomination in the eyes of God. Real worship is to give Christ to God as a present, as a gift, and then to enjoy this gift with God. Hence, Christ is for God and also for us. In our worship we may say, "Father, I offer Your Son as a present for You to enjoy." When we do this, the Father may say, "A portion of this gift is for you and for all your brothers and sisters to enjoy."

THE CENTRAL THOUGHT OF LEVITICUS

The central thought of Leviticus is that the universal, all-inclusive, and inexhaustible Christ is everything to God and to God's people. Today we can speak of the enjoyment of Christ, but one day all things will be headed up in Christ (Eph. 1:10). At that time, Christ will be everything to God and man. The enjoyment of this one person will be the unique celebration in the universe. This wonderful One has thousands of aspects, titles, and names, and every one is for us to enjoy.

THE INEXHAUSTIBLE CHRIST
BEING THE LIFE-GIVING SPIRIT DWELLING IN US

Hebrews 13:21 tells us that God equips us for every good

work in the doing of His will, doing in us that which is well-pleasing in His sight through Jesus Christ. This verse indicates that the great, wonderful, and inexhaustible Christ is now in us. This Christ in us is the life-giving Spirit (1 Cor. 15:45). As the Spirit within us, He is so available and easy to experience. If we would simply pray a little, we would pray ourselves into our spirit to touch this One and enjoy Him. He is inexhaustible yet so available. As we enjoy Him in the above-mentioned aspects, we will be led into the experience of His humanity, His divinity, His death, His resurrection, and His ascension, and we will grow in Him in all these aspects.